Jeff Hanson

[Paintings] (ch 3)

THE LORD'S PRAYER

The Lord's Prayer
The Meaning and Power
of the Prayer Jesus Taught

978-1-7910-2125-2 *Hardcover*
978-1-7910-2126-9 *eBook*
978-1-7910-2127-6 *Large Print*

DVD
978-1-7910-2130-6

Leader Guide
978-1-7910-2128-3
978-1-7910-2129-0 *eBook*

Find out more about
Adam Hamilton's
children's book
*The Most Important
Prayer of All:
Stella Learns the
Lord's Prayer* at
**AdamHamilton.com/
LordsPrayer**

Also by Adam Hamilton

24 Hours That Changed the World

Christianity and World Religions

Creed

Enough

Faithful

Final Words from the Cross

Forgiveness

Half Truths

Incarnation

John

Making Sense of the Bible

Not a Silent Night

Seeing Gray in a World
of Black and White

Simon Peter

The Journey

The Walk

The Way

Words of Life

Why?

For more information, visit AdamHamilton.com.

ADAM HAMILTON

Author of *Creed*, *The Walk*, and *The Journey*

THE LORD'S PRAYER

THE MEANING AND POWER OF THE PRAYER JESUS TAUGHT

Abingdon Press

Nashville

THE LORD'S PRAYER

The Meaning and Power of the Prayer Jesus Taught

Library of Congress Control Number: 2021945161

978-1-7910-2125-2

21 22 23 24 25 26 27 28 29 30 — 10 9 8 7 6 5 4 3 2 1
MANUFACTURED IN THE UNITED STATES OF AMERICA

In memory of my grandmother,
Sarah Loretta Lorson Hamilton,
who first taught me the Lord's Prayer
when I was a small child.

CONTENTS

INTRODUCTION

In Luke 11, one of Jesus's disciples approaches and makes a simple request: "Lord, teach us to pray, just as John [the Baptist] taught his disciples" (v. 1). In response, Jesus teaches the disciples what has become known as the Our Father or the Lord's Prayer. No other prayer is more important to Christians than this prayer. It is the *Lord's* prayer—the prayer he taught us to pray. There are a host of other prayers we overhear Jesus praying in the Gospels, and I'll mention them below. But only with this prayer does Jesus say, "Pray like this."

Each word is saturated with meaning, a meaning that we often miss when we pray it by rote as we gather in our churches for worship. Each of its six petitions (five given by the Lord, one added by the early church) reflects the major themes from Jesus's life and ministry. The prayer is meant by Jesus to shape our lives and, through us, to shape and change the world.

Over the years this prayer has come to mean a great deal to me. I pray it with my church family every weekend in worship. I pray it and meditate upon its words in my morning walks. I pray it together with my seven-year-old granddaughter at bedtime when she spends the night. I've prayed it with broken people sitting in my office. I've prayed it at every wedding I've officiated. I pray it at every hospital call I make. I pray it with the dying, and with their friends and family at each funeral or memorial service.

I once visited a woman in hospice care. Helen hadn't been responsive in hours. Her eyes were closed, her breathing had become more labored, and the hospice nurse said that the end was imminent. She had not spoken since the previous day. I pulled up a chair to the bed, gently took her hand in mine, spoke to her, and also to her family sitting around the room. I reminded her of Christ's love and his promises. I read Scripture to her. And I told her how grateful I was to have been her pastor. I then took anointing oil and, with my thumb, made the sign of the cross upon her forehead, a reminder that she belonged to Christ. Finally, with each of her loved ones touching her, we prayed, giving thanks to God for Helen's life and entrusting her to God's care. At the end of this prayer, I said words I had spoken thousands of times before. "Now, let us join together in the prayer that Jesus taught his disciples to pray saying,

> *Our Father, who art in heaven,*
> *hallowed be thy name.*
> *Thy kingdom come,*
> *thy will be done on earth as it is in heaven.*
> *Give us this day our daily bread.*
> *And forgive us our trespasses,*
> *as we forgive those who trespass against us.*
> *And lead us, not into temptation,*
> *but deliver us from evil.*
> *For thine is the kingdom, and the power, and the glory, forever.*
> *Amen.*

As we concluded, one of her children spoke up and said, "Did you all see that?" Another replied, "Yes, I was watching her. She moved her lips, speaking the Lord's Prayer with us." It was a holy and beautiful moment. These were the last words Helen would attempt to speak before she passed a few minutes later. I've seen this happen again and again. (I'll share another similar story later in the book.) Each time it happens, it reminds me of just how important this prayer is to so many. It is deeply embedded in the hearts and minds of most Christians.

The Prayers Jesus Prayed

We know from the feeding of the multitudes and his meal at the Last Supper that Jesus gave thanks before he ate. In Matthew 11:25-26, we read of a short prayer of praise Jesus offers. In John 11, just before raising Lazarus from the dead, we overhear his prayer of thanks. In the parable of the Pharisee and the tax collector, Jesus commended the lowly tax collector who simply prayed, "God, be merciful to me a sinner" (Luke 18:13 KJV). In John 12, as Jesus approaches Jerusalem knowing he will die there, he prays for God to "glorify your name!" (v. 28).

The entirety of John 17 is a prayer Jesus prayed for his disciples, including his request that "they may be one as we are one" (John 17:21-22 NIV). In the garden of Gethsemane, just hours before his crucifixion, he prayed, "Father, if you are willing, take this cup from me; yet not my will, but yours be done" (Luke 22:42 NIV). And from the cross we recall that he prayed Psalm 22:1 (NIV), "My God, my God, why have you forsaken me," and Psalm 31:5 (NIV), "Into your hands

I commit my spirit." From the cross he also prayed, "Father, forgive them, for they don't know what they're doing" (Luke 23:34). All of these and others are important *precisely because it is Jesus* who prayed them. But nowhere else, aside from the Lord's Prayer, does Jesus say, "Pray like this..." (Matthew 6:9).

Learning the Lord's Prayer

I first learned the Lord's Prayer when I was six or seven. At the time my family was not going to church, but my Roman Catholic grandmother wanted me to know of God's love. When I would stay the night at her house, she would often take me to her Catholic church. We might light a candle, go into the sanctuary to pray, or even play bingo with the nuns on Friday nights. It was she who first taught me to pray the Lord's Prayer.

Several years after I learned the prayer, at bedtime I would look at my clock, and whatever the minute hand, I would pray that many Our Fathers. If the time was 10:56 p.m., I'd pray the Lord's Prayer fifty-six times. I became proficient at saying the prayer quickly, reciting it in ten seconds flat. But the quick recitation, even fifty-six times, did little to connect me to God or to shape my life. I'm guessing you've prayed the Lord's Prayer in worship or with others in much the same way—not really thinking about what you are saying or praying. At one point Jesus, citing Isaiah, speaks of people who worship God with their lips while their hearts are far from God. In some ways, this could describe how many of us pray this important prayer.

And that brings me to the point of this little book. Over the years I've spent a great deal of time studying the Lord's Prayer, poring over it word by word, seeking to understand what Jesus was asking us to pray and why. Since God knows what we need before we ask (Matthew 6:8), this prayer, like all prayer, is less about informing God of things we want or need, and more about shaping our own heart and life.

The more I've studied the Lord's Prayer, the richer and more meaningful it has become for me. I pray it every day. I try not to race through it as I did when I was a boy. There are many times I use it devotionally, spending thirty minutes to an hour praying and meditating upon this prayer, expanding on each of its phrases. In a very real sense, we become what we pray. As we'll see in this book, praying trains our hearts on the things we're praying for, and praying this prayer really does have the power to change us and, through us, the world.

Multiple Versions of the Lord's Prayer?

There are three versions of the Lord's Prayer that came to us from the earliest period of Christianity. We are most familiar with Matthew's account, found in the middle of the Sermon on the Mount (Matthew 6:9-13). The standard English version of that prayer was influenced by William Tyndale's 1525 translation, which in turn shaped the form of the prayer as it appeared in the sixteenth-century *Book of Common Prayer* and finally the King James Version of 1611. Tyndale's version was modified slightly into the version most English-speaking Protestants and Catholics pray today. Let's look at the King James Version side by side with a modern translation of Matthew's version of the Lord's Prayer. Modern versions, in this case, the Common English Bible, are based upon more reliable Greek versions of Matthew's Gospel than were available in 1611[1]:

Our Father which art in heaven, Hallowed be thy name.

Thy kingdom come, Thy will be done in earth, as it is in heaven.

Give us this day our daily bread.

And forgive us our debts, as we forgive our debtors.

And lead us not into temptation, but deliver us from evil: For thine is the kingdom, and the power, and the glory, for ever. Amen.

(KJV)

Our Father who is in heaven, uphold the holiness of your name.

Bring in your kingdom so that your will is done on earth as it's done in heaven.

Give us the bread we need for today.

Forgive us for the ways we have wronged you, just as we also forgive those who have wronged us.

And don't lead us into temptation, but rescue us from the evil one.

(CEB)

In addition to different versions of the Lord's Prayer rendered by various English translations, we have a different version found in Luke's account of the prayer. Here it is from the Common English Bible's translation of Luke 11:2-4:

Father, uphold the holiness of your name.
Bring in your kingdom.
Give us the bread we need for today.
Forgive us our sins,
    for we also forgive everyone who has wronged us.
And don't lead us into temptation.

Notice that neither of these New Testament versions of the prayer, Matthew's or Luke's, includes the traditional closing doxology, "For thine is the kingdom, and the power, and the glory, forever. Amen." A footnote in most modern English Bibles mentions that these words are not found in the earliest and best Greek manuscripts of Matthew's or Luke's account of the prayer but were added by early Christians as a doxology.

The doxology is not regarded as part of the Lord's Prayer by Catholics, but it is included by most Protestant churches.

There is a third version of the Lord's Prayer that comes to us from the early church, in a document called *The Didache* or *The Lord's Teaching Through the Twelve Apostles to the Gentiles*. This is a fascinating document describing the practices of the early church that some scholars believe was written in the first century, and others the second century, offering guidance in the Christian life. In chapter 8 of the *Didache* we find Matthew's version of the prayer quoted.

> *Do not pray as the hypocrites, but as the Lord commanded in his Gospel, pray thus: "Our Father, who art in Heaven, hallowed be thy Name, thy Kingdom come, thy will be done, as in Heaven so also upon earth; give us today our daily bread, and forgive us our debt as we forgive our debtors, and lead us not into trial, but deliver us from the Evil One, for thine is the power and the glory for ever."* **Pray thus three times a day.**[2]

Note that this version included the doxology. Note, too, the closing words that are in bold, "Pray thus three times a day." This is a remarkable testimony to the importance of the Lord's Prayer for early Christians. The *Didache* does not tell us when these three times of prayer should be, but its author likely presupposed the Jewish and early Christian practice of praying in the morning, midday, and afternoon, often thought to be at

9 a.m., noon, and 3 p.m. Regardless of when it was prayed, it is clear that the Lord's Prayer was not reserved solely for prayer during corporate worship on Sunday but was used daily by early Christians.

There is one last prayer I'd like you to be aware of, a Jewish prayer that, in some form, likely predates the Lord's Prayer and that Jesus would have been familiar with. The prayer is called the Qaddish or Kaddish, one portion of which is sometimes called the "half kaddish," and, as you'll see, it resembles the Lord's Prayer:

> *Exalted and hallowed be his great name*
> *in the world which he created according to his will.*
> *May he let his kingdom rule*
> *in your lifetime and in your days and in the lifetime*
> *of the whole house of Israel, speedily and soon.*
> *Praised be his great name from eternity to eternity.*
> *And to this say: Amen.*

I include this prayer for you to notice the similarities and the differences between it and the Lord's Prayer. It is likely that Jesus and many other Jews of his time prayed this prayer. In the Kaddish we find the call for God's name to be hallowed and for God's kingdom to come, and these likely were the foundation upon which Jesus built to give us the Lord's Prayer.

Ora et Labora

There's one final word I'd offer by way of introducing this prayer, and it starts with a question: Why do we pray?

Jesus tells us in introducing the Lord's Prayer that "your Father knows what you need before you ask" (Matthew 6:8b), making clear that we don't pray in order to inform God of anything. Nor do we pray to convince God to do something God does not want to do. My experience in daily prayer the last forty years is that prayer is less about asking God to do something, than it is about expressing our heart to God and opening ourselves to God's will.

It's been said that prayer is to the soul what breathing is to the body. The most basic act of prayer is expressed in two words: *Thank you.* When we're struggling with guilt or shame, our prayer is *Forgive me.* When we're hurting or afraid, it is *Help me.* Daily we might offer our lives to God praying *Use me.*

And when we ask for God's help, or for God to act in some way, how does God typically respond? I have occasionally seen what I believe is a miracle, God's direct intervention suspending the laws of nature to act in response to someone's prayers. But miracles, by definition, are not God's ordinary way of working. *God's primary way of answering prayer is working in and through us and others, empowering us and leading us to action.* Our prayer trains our heart on the object of our concern and, to the degree that we are able, moves us to action.

Ora et labora is a Latin phrase that means "pray and work." It means different things to different people, but to many it captures the idea that prayer serves to move our hearts and to empower and lead us to action. I believe this is a key to understanding the Lord's Prayer.

The prayer is filled with imperatives. We ask God to hallow his name, to make his kingdom come and his will done. We ask God to give us daily bread, to forgive us, to lead us, and to deliver us. Aside from the request for forgiveness, every other petition in this prayer is meant to train our hearts on the object of the request and to *open our hearts so that God may use us to be part of the answer to our prayer.* This idea, that prayer is meant to move us to action, will form a central interpretive principle as we examine each phrase in this prayer.

As we begin our study, let's start by joining together in the prayer Jesus taught his disciples saying . . .

Our Father, who art in heaven, hallowed be thy name.
Thy kingdom come, thy will be done on earth as it is in heaven.
Give us this day our daily bread.
And forgive us our trespasses, as we forgive those who trespass against us.
And lead us, not into temptation, but deliver us from evil.
For thine is the kingdom, and the power, and the glory, forever.
Amen.

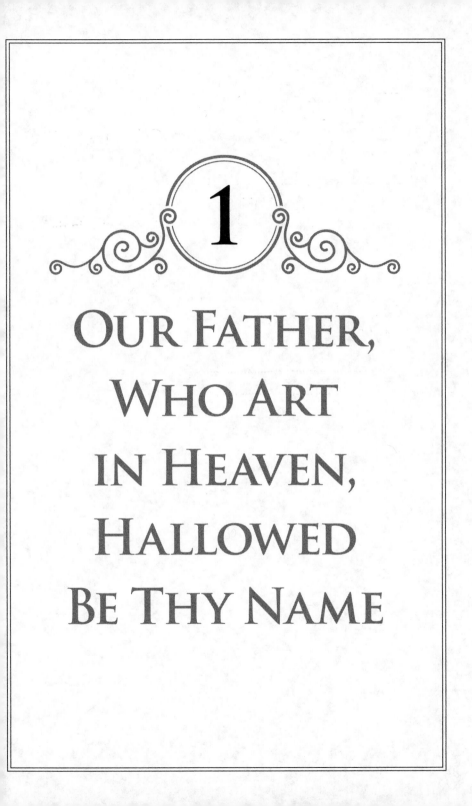

1

Our Father, Who Art in Heaven, Hallowed Be Thy Name

1

Our Father,
Who Art in Heaven,
Hallowed Be
Thy Name

This, then, is how you should pray:

> *"Our Father in heaven,*
> *hallowed be your name,*
> *your kingdom come,*
> *your will be done,*
>   *on earth as it is in heaven.*
> *Give us today our daily bread.*
> *And forgive us our debts,*
>   *as we also have forgiven our debtors.*
> *And lead us not into temptation,*
>   *but deliver us from the evil one."*
>
>   *—Matthew 6:9-13 (NIV)*

During the week that I wrote this chapter, I prayed the Lord's Prayer in a funeral, in a wedding, in my own private prayer time, and in each of our worship services at the Church of the Resurrection.

While I first learned this prayer from my Catholic grandmother when I was six or seven, it was in hearing the prayer prayed every week in church as a child that it was etched in my memory. In most mainline churches, the Lord's Prayer comes at the conclusion of the pastoral prayer, which the pastor prays on behalf of the congregation. Just before the conclusion to the pastoral prayer, the pastor will say something like, "Now, let us join together in the prayer that Jesus taught his disciples, saying…"

The words that Jesus gave his disciples (and us) form the best known and most often prayed prayer in the world. Yet, despite our familiarity with this prayer, and the frequency with which we may pray it, we often fail to grasp its meaning. We know it, but often we don't *know* it. We pray it, but all too often we don't actually *pray* it.

Some years ago, friends took us to dinner at a fancy restaurant. I've eaten in plenty of restaurants, but felt utterly confused by the panoply of silverware, the French words on the menu, and the multiple courses of small dishes that were so elegantly served. The saving grace was the sous-chef who accompanied the wait staff at the presentation of each course, who briefly described each dish, how it was prepared, and what to note as we ate. As a result of his explanation, we savored every bite. But without the explanation, we would have missed out on so much.

Likewise, a few years ago I took my daughters to a Kansas City Chiefs football game. One of them had never followed football and knew nothing about the rules, strategies, or play. It was confusing to her at first, but as play progressed, I explained the game and the more she learned, the more excited she became until, at the end of the game when the Chiefs had won, she was cheering like a long-time fan and asked when she could come again.

Learning to pray the Lord's Prayer is a bit like learning how to appreciate a meal at a fine French restaurant or understanding how a professional football game is played. You can devour the meal quickly, like a meal at McDonald's—pass the catsup, please—and it will still nourish you. You can have fun at a pro football game and enjoy the atmosphere even if you don't follow the game. But both mean so much more when you actually understand what you are eating or have a grasp of the way the game is played. In the same way, the Lord's Prayer begs to be explored, understood, engaged, and savored. There is so much more here than we might at first grasp. I'm hoping this book serves the role the sous-chef played at our meal or that I played for my daughter at the football game. When you are finished reading this book, I believe you'll pray this prayer differently, with greater meaning, and that its words will deepen and shape your faith, your heart, and your life.

In each chapter we'll focus on one line from the prayer. If you are reading this book with others, a chapter a week, I hope you'll focus on that one line you're studying every day that week. With this in mind, let's turn to the prayer's first line: **"Our Father, who art in heaven, hallowed be thy name."**

Our Father

There are many names or titles used to address God in Scripture. You've likely heard of a few of these names, names like El (God), or El Elyon (God Most High), or El Shaddai (God Almighty), or Adonai (Lord), or Yahweh (I Am that I Am or I Am the Source and Sustainer of Life, but most often displayed in English translations as LORD in all caps)—Yahweh appears over six thousand times in one form or another in the Hebrew Bible/Old Testament. My Jewish friends often address their prayers to "Lord our God, Ruler [or King] of the Universe."

Yet when Jesus taught his disciples to pray, he taught them to address God in a way that appears only rarely in the Hebrew Bible. He taught them to address God as "Our Father." Like the fine French meal, there's more here than meets the eye.

First, when teaching his disciples to pray, Jesus didn't ask them to pray to "My Father" but *Our* Father." This is significant. We might pray this prayer alone, but as we do, we still pray to *our* Father, asking him to give *us* this day *our* daily, to forgive *us* as *we* forgive, to lead *us* not into temptation, but to deliver *us* from evil. I believe Jesus intended that this prayer stand in stark contrast to our natural tendency to "look out for number one"—to care primarily about the self. We live in a world that is focused on *my*, *mine*, and *me*, but Jesus teaches us to pray *our*, *us*, and *we*.

Jesus often spoke of God simply as Father, or as my Father. We may of course pray this way as well. But when Jesus gave this particular prayer, he was inviting his disciples to pray not only for ourselves, *but also for the world around us*. The prayer reminds us that Christian faith is not meant to be lived alone, but in community. Jesus began his ministry with a small group of twelve disciples. He organized a church—a community of people seeking to follow him *together*. The prayer reminds us that our faith is intended to be lived out *with others*, and that our prayers are prayed with others and *for others*.

> The prayer reminds us that our faith is intended to be lived out *with others*, and that our prayers are prayed with others and *for others*.

When I pray this line of the prayer, I put a special emphasis on the word *our* as a way of reminding myself that God is not simply my Father, but he is the God and Father of *us all*. Whether others acknowledge him or not, he is still the Creator of all things, the Giver and Sustainer of all life. He is the Father of all humans. This seems particularly important in a world prone to polarization and divisions. God is not simply the God of Protestants but also of Catholics and Orthodox believers. God is not simply the God of conservatives, but also of liberals. God is not the Father of any one nation, or ethnic group, but the Father of all nations and peoples. He is not merely the Father of Christians, but the Father of Jews, Muslims, Hindus, Buddhists, and even atheists and agnostics who don't believe in him!

7

And yes, in our politically divided times, to pray "our Father" is also to recognize that God is the God and Father of the Republicans and the Democrats, liberals and conservatives. If you share the same Father, you are family with these others. To acknowledge God as our common Father is to recognize our obligation to our neighbors, all of whom are made in the likeness and image of God. We'll come back to this theme in chapter three.

————————————

Let's consider for a few minutes that Jesus teaches us to pray to our *Father*. I'm writing the final revisions of this chapter on Father's Day. The challenge for every preacher preaching on Father's Day (and Mother's Day too) is that congregation members have such different experiences with their fathers. Some had dads who were amazing—present, protective, loving, and involved in their children's lives. Others had dads who were just average. And some had fathers who were absent, emotionally distant, or worse, emotionally or physically abusive. The rising divorce rates starting in the 1960s played a part in the complicated relationships many have with their dads.

I have met many people whose experience of their earthly father was painful. They had fathers who were physically or emotionally absent or abusive, or who otherwise made it hard for them to use the imagery of father to represent God, and when they do use this language, they find it hard to believe that God is loving, kind, and can be trusted.

Roberta Bondi, who taught church history at Emory's Candler School of Theology, wrote,

> I...[grew] up in the forties and fifties with a loving but authoritarian, perfectionistic father who left the family when I was eleven. Like many other people, having transferred to God the Father all the pain I felt around my human father, I simply couldn't get past the father language of the prayer to reach God....I was hurting so much and so mistrustful of God.[1]

Ultimately, at that time in her life, Roberta substituted the word *Parent* for *Father*.

Knowing this, I wonder if Jesus intentionally chose this image of Father, not because God is like our earthly fathers, but because so many long for the love of a father they never had. Your earthly father is not the pattern for God's fatherhood, but *God is the pattern and example of what a father is meant to be*; that is, one who is steadfast, faithful, loving, kind, compassionate, merciful, and present. In this, the words of Jesus are instructive.

As my children were growing up, and still to the present day, I pray that I might, by my love for them, help them see a glimpse of the love of their Father in heaven. Here it is important to recognize that earthly fathers are not the pattern of what it means to call God Father. God is the pattern earthly fathers should seek to emulate as they seek to be fathers.

At the same time, Roberta Bondi is right to recognize that God transcends both male and female, and that both fathering and mothering are a part of God's nature and character. When Genesis 1:27 describes God's creation of humanity, the text says, "In the image of God he created them; male and female he created them" (Genesis 1:27b NIV). If both male and female were created in the image of God, then God must possess both masculine and feminine dimensions. We catch glimpses of the feminine imagery applied to God on occasion in Scripture. In Isaiah 66:13 we read, "As a mother comforts her child, / so I will comfort you." In multiple passages the metaphor of giving birth is applied to God and God's work, as in Deuteronomy 32:18b, "You forgot the God who gave birth to you." We see this in the New Testament's imagery of being "born of God" or "born again." Childbirth is clearly a feminine metaphor applied to God. Jesus draws upon the idea of a hen caring for her chicks when speaking of his concern for Jerusalem and her people. The Bible clearly recognizes both masculine and feminine dimensions of God.

Ultimately all of our language about God is anthropomorphic, making use of human metaphors so that we can comprehend the God who is beyond our comprehension. God transcends all of our metaphors, yet they are helpful in allowing us to know God and to relate to God. But there was clearly something important to Jesus about the metaphor of Father when it came to his relationship with God. It is used more often by him than any other form of address.

When I address God as Father, I think of my relationship with my daughters and now my seven-year-old granddaughter. Before my daughters were born, I did not know I could love another human being so deeply. As they were growing up, I was not the perfect father, but I loved, and continue to love, my daughters fiercely. I wanted to give them everything I possibly could to help them have a good and joyful life. When their hearts broke, my heart broke (and still does when they are hurt). When they acted to care for others, I felt pride in their character and their selfless acts. I feel great joy when they talk with me, want to spend time with me, when they share their lives with me. I have told them, and really believe it, that I would freely give my life to save or rescue them. That's what I think of when Jesus says, "Pray like this, 'Our Father…'"

Recently I walked into my granddaughter, Stella's, bedroom and laid down next to her, and she said, "Papa, can you just stay here with me and hold me as I go to sleep?" I put my arm around her and choked back the tears, knowing in a couple of years she'll not ask me to do this anymore. But for that moment I savored holding her until she went to sleep. That, too, is what I think of when I pray, "Our Father…"

I appreciated something that Pope Francis said in his book on the Lord's Prayer. He noted that, when we address God as "Our Father," we are invited to remember that, regardless of whether our human fathers loved us deeply or abandoned us entirely, or whether our fathers died or were simply absentee, *we are not orphans*. In fact, there are no orphans, for we all have a Father who loves us.

For me, when Jesus invites us to pray "Our Father," these are the things I think about. God is Father to you in a way your earthly father may never have been. At the same time, it may be more helpful for you to imagine God as a nurturing and tender Mother, for God is surely that too. Or more broadly, as Roberta Bondi does, to think of God as our Parent.

Who Art in Heaven

I've been asked on many occasions by children, "Where does God live?" It's a great question. Where *does* God live? In this prayer Jesus addresses God as Our Father, who art in heaven. Luke does not include these words in his version of the Lord's Prayer. Matthew does. Let's consider the meaning of heaven in Scripture.

From what we can tell, the ancient Hebrews imagined the earth as the center of the universe. Land masses were surrounded by water. Below the earth was the underworld where the dead resided and far below that were more waters— "the deep"—upon which the land rested. A dome encapsulated our atmosphere and near the top of that dome the sun, moon, and stars traveled across the sky. Above this was more water held back by some kind of solid layer whose gates could be opened, allowing the rains to fall to the earth. Finally, above that, were the "highest heavens." In the Greek language the New Testament was written in, the word for heaven is *ouranos* from which we have our word, Uranus, the seventh planet from the sun. Ouranos or Uranus was, in Greek mythology, the god of the sky.

At times, the word *ouranos*—heaven—was used to describe everything between the ground and the dome above: the unseen atmosphere, the air we breathe, the place where the birds of the air take their flight. But it is distinct from the earth, which refers to both the physical, visible world and the realm in which humans have dominion and often live lives of alienation from God.

When heaven and Father are combined in Matthew, as in the opening of our prayer, Matthew uses the plural *ouronois*, heavens. Heaven, or heavens, in this sense, is distinct from earth, the material world, and yet it envelops both. Like the air or atmosphere or even wind, we cannot see it, but we breathe it and at times feel it. We are therefore surrounded by heaven. The point I want you to note is that heaven isn't always "up there" or "out there" in Scripture; it is also all that is around us even though we can't see it. In this sense, *God is as near as the air that we breathe.*

Heaven isn't always "up there" or "out there" in Scripture; it is also all that is around us even though we can't see it. . . . *God is as near as the air that we breathe.*

But *ouranos* also meant specifically that region where the sun, moon, and stars "trace their courses above." So, Psalm 19 begins, "Heaven is declaring God's glory; / the sky is proclaiming his handiwork." In this sense, Jesus invites us also to understand that God's glory and presence permeates *all that exists beyond the earth's atmosphere.*

Today we understand just how vast the heavens are. Unlike the ancients, we know the earth is round, it revolves on its axis every twenty-four hours, and travels around the sun in a 365-day orbit, hurling through space at a speed of about 67,000 miles per hour. Our sun is but one of about one hundred billion stars in our Milky Way galaxy, all revolving around a black hole at the center. And our galaxy is but one of perhaps two trillion galaxies moving away from a common point of origin in a universe that's about 93 billion light years across (it would take a photon of light, traveling at 186,000 miles per second, approximately 93 billion years to cross that distance). And God not only permeates this universe, God stands outside and beyond it.

Listen to how Isaiah captures this in Isaiah 40:26, "Look up at the sky and consider: / Who created these? / The one who brings out their attendants one by one, / summoning each of them by name." God is as near as the air we breathe, yet God's presence permeates and extends beyond the vastness of space so that we might say not merely that he has "the whole world in his hands," but the entire universe in his hands! In this sense we pray, "Our Father, whose glory fills the universe and beyond!"

For Jesus, "heaven" is most often used to represent God's reign, the world as it was meant to be, hence the frequent use of the phrase "the kingdom of heaven" in Matthew's Gospel. In this case, it is usually the plural form of the word *ouranos*, so "heavens" might be a better translation. While it might include all that is below, it most often seems to indicate the realm where God's will is done, where injustice, poverty, cruelty, inhumanity, violence, corruption, and pain have been banished. We'll consider this more fully in the next chapter when we turn to Jesus's words, "Thy kingdom come, thy will be done on earth as it is in heaven."

Finally, heaven is used in Scripture to describe the future state and place where the righteous dead dwell with God (Matthew 8:10-11). Jesus promises he will go and prepare a place for us there, and that in his Father's house there is "room to spare" (John 14:1-3). First-century Jewish and Christian understandings of the afterlife were more complex than simply going to heaven after death. We'll consider this in more detail in the next chapter as well. Heaven, for early Christians, came to encompass the place where the saints dwelt with God, where death had been vanquished, and which one day would come on earth.

Where is God? He is as near as the air that we breathe. His presence permeates the cosmos. He is even in the realm of the dead. The various ways in which *heaven* is used in Scripture points to the truth that there is nowhere that we can go where God is not. I love how Psalm 139 captures it when the psalmist asks,

> *Where could I go to get away from your spirit?*
> *Where could I go to escape your presence?*
> *If I went up to heaven, you would be there.*
> *If I went down to the grave, you would be there too!*
> *If I could fly on the wings of dawn,*
> *stopping to rest only on the far side of the ocean—*
> *even there your hand would guide me;*
> *even there your strong hand would hold me tight!*
> *(Psalm 139:7-10)*

This is why Paul could say with assurance, "Nothing can separate us from God's love in Christ Jesus our Lord: not death or life, not angels or rulers, not present things or future things, not powers or height or depth, or any other thing that is created" (Romans 8:38-39).

Our Father, whose glory fills the heavenly realms, whose presence permeates the deepest depths, who is as near as the air that I breathe, who is with my loved ones who have died, who rules over all...

Hallowed Be Thy Name

Finally, we come to the first request or petition of the Lord's Prayer: Hallowed be thy name. What is missed in most English translations is that this is a request for *God* to act: Our Father, who art in heaven, hallow your name! What are we asking for in this petition, and why?

I mentioned in the introduction that one Jewish prayer that dates back to the time of Jesus is called the Kaddish. It likely began as a kind of doxology or word of praise to God that was recited following a rabbi's teaching on the Torah. Centuries later it became used as words of praise at the death of a loved one. It seems from reading the Lord's Prayer that Jesus was familiar with an early version of the Kaddish with its opening petition concerning God, *May His great name be hallowed in the world which He created.*

Hallowed is not a word we use often today. Occasionally we might hear someone say of a particular place, "this is hallowed ground." We hear the word most around the end of October when we prepare for Halloween. Halloween is the e'en (evening before) All-Hallow's day. What is a hallow? It is someone or something that is holy—and *holy* comes from the Old English word *halga*, which originally came from the Greek word for holy, *hagios*. The Hebrew word is *qadosh* (sometimes spelled with a *k*), which has the same root meaning as *kaddish*, the name of the ancient Jewish prayer with striking similarities to the Lord's Prayer. The Latin word for *hallow* is *sanctus* from which we have our word "sanctify."

To be hallowed or holy is be set apart for God and for God's purposes. It is the association with God that makes a person, place, or thing holy. *Hallow* can also mean pure, or that which is wholly different from the ordinary. It can signify something or someone that is cleansed, purified, righteous, or utterly good. Finally, it can mean "revered or something that inspires awe" (one part of the Greek root word means to "shrink back from").

The Hebrew and Greek words for *holy* appear over nine hundred times in Scripture. In the Creation story God sets apart the seventh day, the Sabbath, as holy, a day that belongs to God and is not to be treated as any ordinary day. When Moses heard God speak through the burning bush, the voice said to him, "Take off your sandals, because you are standing on holy ground" (Exodus 3:5). Aaron, Moses's brother, was to wear a turban with an ornament on the front that said, "Holy to the Lord," meaning that as priest, he had been dedicated to God and God's service (Exodus 28:36). The Temple was called holy. So were the furnishings in it. Israel was called God's holy people (see Exodus 19:6). And God said to them, "Be holy, for I am holy" (Leviticus 11:44, 45 NRSV).

In the prayer that Jesus taught us, we are asking God to hallow or make holy God's *name*. When Scripture speaks of

God's name, it is often a way of speaking of God or of God's reputation. I recall a man who was slandered and falsely accused of something. He sought to "clear his name" and noted, when he challenged the one who had spoken falsely of him, "All I have is my name," by which he meant his reputation.

But how does God hallow God's own name? Here I would remind you of the premise I mentioned earlier regarding prayer: When we pray, we fix our heart on the things we pray for, and we invite God to work through us and others to answer our prayers. In this case, to pray for God to hallow God's name is to desire that God's name be hallowed; and as we desire it, we invite God to use us to hallow God's name.

We hallow God's name in our praise, in the honor we show God; but, perhaps preeminently, we hallow God's name by living in a way that reflects God's goodness, majesty, beauty, and love. All creation is meant to hallow God's name, to bring God glory and honor.

We hallow God's name by living in a way that reflects God's goodness, majesty, beauty, and love.

Among my favorite places in the world is the Pacific Coast; I am enamored with the rugged beauty where mountains meet the sea. I love to walk the beach listening to the sound of the waves crashing against the shore or watch them break against the rock formations scattered along the coastline from Washington State all the way to Mexico. On our last trip to the Pacific, the humpbacks were migrating and calving. I'd never seen so many of these magnificent creatures; pods were swimming by just off the shore. It was awesome. The waves, the whales, the sunsets, they all displayed the glory of God. By simply being, they hallow God's name.

When we pray for God to hallow God's name, we are praying, "May your name be hallowed in and through us—in our lives, our words, our thoughts, our actions." When I was a teen there was a song we used to sing in youth group, that contained the words, "In my life, Lord, be glorified...today." That is what we are inviting God to do as we pray, "hallowed be thy name."

In many ways, the prayer to hallow God's name is the positive side of the Third Commandment, "Do not use the Lord your God's name as if it were of no significance" (Exodus 20:7) or, as many of us memorized it, "Thou shalt not take the name of the Lord thy God in vain" (KJV). In our lives we either misuse and denigrate God's name, or we hallow God's name by what we say and how we live our lives.

Today there are an increasing number of people who have been repelled by Christianity because of Christians they have known, or witnessed, acting in ways that did not hallow God's name. They have at times experienced Christians who were unkind, judgmental, self-centered, materialistic, insensitive, racist, and more.

Several years ago, I watched a film about religious leaders who sexually abused children, as many as one thousand of them, over a period of seventy years. As the credits rolled, they listed the number of cases and locations and I found myself weeping in the theater. These actions inflicted profound pain and suffering on these children and their families. And in the process, they profaned God's name.

While this is a most egregious example, there are so many others. There are everyday Christians who act in unchristian ways. So many times, I've met people who can recount the hurt they have experienced at the hands of Christians, or ways in which vocal Christians they've known stood for values that seemed the antithesis of right and just. How many times I've heard people say, "If that's what God-followers are like, you can keep your religion, because I'm not interested." The truth is, every Christian at some point profanes God's name.

But if people profane God's name, it is also true that people can hallow God's name. I'll say it again: when you pray this part of the Lord's Prayer, you are not only seeking to hallow God's name, you are also praying, "Father, *use me* to hallow your name. Help me to show others who you are. Help *me* to love them with your love. Help *me* to keep your name holy."

Bernie Haldiman grew up in the Methodist Church. He spent his career working in the field of technology, developing quartz crystals used in communications, sonar, and computers, eventually retiring at the age of fifty-one as the vice president of his company. He didn't stay retired, though. He wanted to use all that he knew about technology and math to help others, so he got his teaching certificate and went back to work as a math and computer science teacher in an inner-city high school. While doing this, he began volunteering in our computer ministry at Church of the Resurrection. This ministry receives donated computers from various businesses and individuals, updates the hard drives, memory, processors, and software, then installs them in nonprofit organizations that otherwise could not afford them. This includes urban schools both in the Kansas City area as well as in Honduras, Haiti, and various countries in Africa. The team calls themselves "Geeks for God." Bernie tirelessly served in this ministry, helping drive this work.

Bernie died recently of pancreatic cancer. I had the honor of preaching the message at his funeral. I titled the message, "The Gospel According to Bernie," because Bernie didn't just talk about the gospel, he lived it. Bernie had prayed the Lord's Prayer thousands of times across the course of his life. I prayed it with him and his wife, Connie, as we recommitted his life to Christ shortly before his death. But he not only prayed this prayer, he lived it. He knew that God was not only his Father, but *our* Father—the Father of all those teenagers at urban high schools. God was Father to the children in Mooiplaas, a community of 16,000 people living in shacks built at the base of a huge trash dump in South Africa, where children use computers Bernie prepared for them. God is Father of the children in the Juan Wesley School in Honduras and of the formerly homeless people making a new start at Avenue of Life in Kansas City, all of whom had a chance for a future with hope in part because of Bernie's work. Bernie knew that God not only dwells up there or out there, but God is as close as the air that we breathe. Bernie didn't simply pray for God to hallow God's name; he sought to live in such a way that God's name was hallowed and people could see God's mercy, compassion, and love through him.

I'd end with one final example of hallowing God's name. I received a note recently from one of our church members. She told me how she'd been shopping at Target, buying uniforms and school supplies for the students at area schools we partner with, schools that serve the most under-resourced communities in Kansas City. We provide tutoring, books, school supplies, and uniforms. This woman wrote to say that as she went through the checkout line at Target, the cashier asked why she was buying so many uniforms and school supplies. She explained to the cashier about our church's school partnerships. She did not mention our church by name, but the cashier said, "You go to the Church of the Resurrection, don't you?"

"Yes," the church member replied. "Do you attend Resurrection too?"

"No, not yet," answered the cashier, "but I've met so many of your members coming through here buying uniforms and school supplies, they are all so friendly, and I love that they are buying uniforms for children who need them. That's got me thinking that I need to get back to church and that I'd like to attend your church when I do."

This woman knew nothing about our building, our denomination, or our doctrines. Everything she knew about the congregation was encompassed in her interactions with members who had come to Target to help others who needed their support. That is what drew her to want to visit—to "come and see," as Jesus invited his first two disciples. She had met people who hallowed God's name.

In your life, are you hallowing God's name? What do others know of God by watching you?

Every week in worship, somewhere in the middle of the service, one of our pastors leads the congregation in saying the Lord's Prayer. Our people pray together, "Our Father, who art in heaven, hallowed be thy name..." And at the end of the service, I raise my hands over the congregation to give them the benediction, the final charge and sending forth. Their eyes are closed, and as I speak the words, I push my hands forward as though I'm thrusting these members out into the world that they might go to hallow God's name by their words and actions.

God is the Father, the Source, Protector, Lover, of *all of us*. God holds the entire universe in God's hands but is as near as the air that we breathe. And we're meant to live our lives in such a way that God hallows God's name through us.

As we end this chapter, let's join together in the prayer that Jesus taught his disciples saying,

> *Our Father, who art in heaven, hallowed be thy name.*
> *Thy kingdom come, thy will be done on earth as it is in heaven.*
> *Give us this day our daily bread.*
> *And forgive us our trespasses, as we forgive those who trespass against us.*
> *And lead us, not into temptation, but deliver us from evil.*
> *For thine is the kingdom, and the power, and the glory, forever.*
> *Amen.*

WHOSE
WILL BE
DONE?

2

WHOSE WILL
BE DONE?

After this manner, therefore, pray ye: Our Father which art in heaven, Hallowed be thy name.

Thy kingdom come, Thy will be done in earth, as it is in heaven.
(Matthew 6:9-10 KJV)

[Jesus] withdrew from them about a stone's throw, knelt down, and prayed. He said, "Father, if it's your will, take this cup of suffering away from me. However, not my will but your will must be done."

(Luke 22:41-42)

As we continue our study of the Lord's Prayer, I'm reminded of a story I once heard about a Republican and a Democratic candidate for office who were meeting in a town hall debate. In the course of the discussion, the subject of religion came up. The Republican candidate said to the Democrat, "I'll bet you $20 you don't even know the words to the Lord's Prayer."

The Democrat responded, "I'll take your bet. I do know the words to the Lord's Prayer."

"Great," the Republican replied, "Let's hear it." The Democrat responded, "Now I lay me down to sleep, I pray the Lord my soul to keep…" The Republican looked stunned, and then took out his billfold and handed his opponent $20, saying, "I can't believe you actually knew it!"

It's an old joke. But it points to the struggle that many people have with this prayer—not simply forgetting the words to the Lord's Prayer, but even if they remember them, not fully comprehending their meaning. That's particularly true in the second line of the Lord's Prayer, "Thy kingdom come, thy will be done on earth as it is in heaven."

This is one of the most important lines in the entire prayer. Father Daniel Harrington, a Jesuit scholar, notes that in this petition we find the "central concern" of the entire Lord's Prayer.[1] In fact, it is the central concern of Jesus's entire ministry. His teaching, life, death, and resurrection focused on announcing God's kingdom, inviting people to be a part of it, and encouraging people to not only pray, but to live in such a way that God's kingdom comes on earth as it is in heaven.

Mine or Thine?

I'm grateful that we continue to pray the Lord's Prayer in the "King's English" that includes "Thy" and "Thine." We know the words mean *you* and *yours*, but I love the poetry of "Thy" and "Thine" as they rhyme with their antonyms, "my" and "mine." As we pray the second line of the prayer we come to a moment of decision: my and mine or Thy and Thine?

In each line of the Lord's Prayer, there is some word or phrase that I give special emphasis to as I pray. That is particularly true when I come to the words *Thy* or *Thine* in the Lord's Prayer. In saying these words, I am making an intentional choice as I pray. I am praying *Thy* and *Thine*, Lord, not my and mine. *Thy* name, not my name, be hallowed. *Thy* kingdom come, not my kingdom come. *Thy* will, not mine, be done. And, as we'll see in the last chapter, when I come to the doxology of the Lord's Prayer, I pray, *Thine*, not mine, is the kingdom; *Thine*, not mine, is the power; *Thine*, not mine, is the glory.

Remember, when we pray, we fix our hearts on what we pray.

Remember, when we pray, we fix our hearts on what we pray. As I pray these words, I'm training my heart to think less of myself, what I want, the hallowing of my name, my little kingdom, and my power and glory. Instead, I yield all of these things to God. Try praying this excerpt from the Lord's Prayer now, giving emphasis to each italicized word, and see if you sense what I'm talking about:

> Our Father, who art in heaven, hallowed be *thy* name.
> *Thy* kingdom come. *Thy* will be done... *Thine* is
> the kingdom. *Thine* is the power. *Thine* is the glory,
> forever, Amen.

Not my or mine, but Thy and Thine.

This is the essence of what it means to call Jesus Lord. The word *Lord* signifies one in authority over another. It is what it means to recognize that "God is God, and I am not." With these little words we pray, "less of me and more of thee." We yield to God's will, and we seek God's glory and honor before our own. Can you begin to see the power of praying this prayer daily, or as the early church did, three times each day? How dramatically our lives change when we're not focused on getting our way, building our kingdoms, striving for our glory. Every part of our lives is better when we live "not my and mine but Thy and Thine."

To be authentically human, to be the people God made us to be, is to seek the hallowing of God's name, the coming of God's kingdom, and the doing of God's will. By praying the words of this prayer, we are submitting to God's kingdom, rule, and reign, and to the Lordship of Jesus Christ.

By the way, among the first words we seem to learn as children is "mine." I remember each of my daughters learning to play with other children when they were just toddlers. When one child would pick up a toy, suddenly the other wanted it, would grab it, and say, "Mine!" The first child would either start crying, or grab it back and say, "Mine!" That seems to be how we're wired, and though we become more discreet about it as we grow up, we continue to struggle with the "my and mine syndrome" our entire lives. The Lord's Prayer is an antidote for this soul disease.

Thy Kingdom Come, Thy Will be Done

Thy *kingdom* come. The focus of Jesus's preaching and teaching was what he called the kingdom of God, or in Matthew's Gospel, the kingdom of heaven. Jesus mentions the Kingdom more than one hundred times. You cannot fully understand Jesus, what he taught, stood for, and incarnated without understanding the kingdom of heaven.

Like all words about God, *kingdom* is a metaphor. Jesus, and all people speaking about God, used analogies, similes, and metaphors to describe God, God's will, and God's ways. Part of the challenge with Jesus's words about the Kingdom, for us, is that most of us don't live in kingdoms, but instead in representative democracies. We have to work a bit to understand the metaphor.

In Jesus's day a kingdom or empire was a geographic region or realm ruled over by a king or an emperor. A benevolent king or queen sought to govern with justice, to rule with righteousness and mercy, and in a way that served the common good. In turn the king or queen's authority was respected, their rules obeyed, and they were honored. People knelt before them. They hailed them as royalty. They recognized their ultimate authority.

It's helpful to remember, when we consider this idea of kingdom, where Scripture begins. "In the beginning God created the heavens and the earth" (Genesis 1:1 NIV). The entire cosmos is God's handiwork. Consequently, God is the rightful ruler of it all. The universe itself is God's kingdom. This is why several common Jewish blessings begin, *Barukh atah Adonai Eloihenu Melek ha Olam*—"Blessed are you, Lord our God, King of the Universe." God is the ruler or king of the universe, and the entire cosmos is God's realm or kingdom.

Why then do we need to pray for God's kingdom to come? Isn't it already here?

In Genesis 1:28, after creating humans, God said to them, "Be fertile and multiply; fill the earth and master it. Take charge of the fish of the sea, the birds in the sky, and everything crawling on the ground." The Hebrew word for "master it" signifies gaining control over the earth. And the Hebrew word for "take charge" signifies ruling or having dominion over something. Here, as the Bible begins, God gives humans the authority to rule over this planet on God's behalf.

Much of the rest of the Bible, and of human history for that matter, is the story of the many ways humans can make a mess of things. Beginning in Genesis 3, Adam and Eve turn away from God's will by eating forbidden fruit. A chapter later Cain kills his brother Abel. In the next chapter Lamech kills a man. And by Genesis 6, the earth is so filled with violence that God grieves that he even made human beings and believes he must end the experiment with a flood and start over. That's just the first six chapters of the Bible.

These stories are not told in Scripture to recount ancient history, but to teach us about ourselves. We can be a violent race. In the last century over one hundred million people died as a result of war. Millions more died from starvation and malnutrition-related diseases that could have been avoided, while millions of others across our planet struggle with obesity. Nearly sixty years after the Civil Rights Acts of the 1960s, racism continues to impact our world. And that doesn't begin to name the many personal demons we wrestle with: pride, indifference, addiction, deceitfulness, materialism, and many more. Beneath all of these is often idolatry, allowing something else to sit on the throne of our heart and life, to be our god or king.

And in response to all of this, Jesus tells us to pray "Thy kingdom come."

Some see the Lord's Prayer as originally being composed using a poetic structure, like the Psalms. In Hebrew poetry, the first phrase or line in a couplet is restated and expanded in the second line. We see that in this portion of our prayer:

> *Thy kingdom come,*
> *thy will be done*
> *on earth as it is in heaven.*

The second line clarifies and expands upon the first, and what I've shown above as the third line helps define both of the lines before it. What are we praying when we pray for God's kingdom to come? We are praying for God's will to be done on earth as it is in heaven.

Why do we have to pray for God's kingdom to come and God's will to be done? Because, despite the fact that God is the "King of the Universe," humans continue to follow Adam and Eve's lead in being drawn at times to act in ways that are not in keeping with God's will. The apostle Paul captured this well in Romans 7:18-19 when he wrote, "The desire to do good is inside of me, but I can't do it. I don't do the good that I want to do, but I do the evil that I don't want to do." This is our struggle, and this is why the Lord's Prayer is so important. It trains my heart and mind on this idea: Thy kingdom come, Thy will be done, on earth as it is in heaven.

The Kingdom of Heaven Has Come Near

When Jesus began his public ministry, this was his message: "Repent, for the kingdom of heaven has come near" (Matthew

4:17 NRSV). God's invisible realm where his will is done was breaking into our visible world as Jesus preached and ministered. As we learned in the last chapter, heaven, *ouronos*, is sometimes used in Scripture to describe God's invisible realm. Jesus came not only announcing God's heavenly kingdom was coming near; he literally embodied the Kingdom.

He healed the sick, forgave sinners, fed the hungry, and raised the dead; and in doing this, Jesus gave us a glimpse of heaven here on earth. You've likely heard it said that Christians are often fixated on getting people to heaven, but Jesus seemed focused on unleashing heaven here on earth. The kingdom of heaven has come near!

As an aside, it might be helpful to note a word about why Matthew uses "kingdom of heaven" where Mark and Luke use "kingdom of God." For years it was taught that this was due to Matthew's Jewish audience who so revered God's name that Matthew substituted the word *heaven* for the word *God* in response. New Testament scholar Jonathan Pennington notes that this is not likely the case. Matthew uses the word *theos*—God—fifty-one times in the Gospel even after rendering "kingdom of God" as "kingdom of heaven." Instead, Pennington proposes that "Matthew is repeatedly setting up a *contrast* between two realms—the heavenly and the earthly—which stand for God on the one hand, and humanity on the other."[2]

In Jesus, and in the lives of all who follow him, the heavenly realm is breaking into the earthly realm. When we "repent" as Jesus called his hearers to do, we have a change of mind that leads to a change of heart and ultimately a change of behavior.

When we pray "Thy" not "my," and we yield ourselves to God, seeking to live as citizens of the Kingdom, God's kingdom does in fact come on earth as it is in heaven.

Every person who chooses to yield her or his life to God, who chooses to follow Jesus, begins to live in the kingdom of heaven, even as each one simultaneously lives in this present earthly realm. We become citizens of two kingdoms. I love how Jesus said it in Luke 17:20-21, "The kingdom of God is not coming with things that can be observed; nor will they say, 'Look, here it is!' or 'There it is!' For, in fact, the kingdom of God is among you" (NRSV). While the Kingdom comes in ways that cannot be observed, once we become a part of the kingdom of God, yielding our lives to him, the Kingdom becomes visible through our lives.

> Each time we pray the Lord's Prayer with meaning, we are yielding our lives to God's will.

Each time we pray the Lord's Prayer with meaning, we are yielding our lives to God's will and in some small way the Kingdom is coming on earth as it is in heaven. In praying this prayer we not only fix our hearts and minds on God's kingdom coming, but we also invite God to use us as instruments to fulfill our prayer. We're praying, in part, "Here I am, Lord, use me."

Glimpses of the Kingdom
of Heaven on Earth

The prophets imagined what it would look like when God's kingdom comes on earth as it is in heaven. Isaiah offers this picture of the heavenly or peaceable kingdom:

> *The wolf will live with the lamb,*
> *and the leopard will lie down with the young goat;*
> *the calf and the young lion will feed together,*
> *and a little child will lead them.*
> *The cow and the bear will graze,*
> *Their young will lie down together,*
> *and a lion eat straw like an ox.*
> *A nursing child will play over the snake's hole;*
> *toddlers will reach right over the serpent's den.*
> *They won't harm or destroy anywhere on my holy mountain;.*
> *The earth will surely be filled with the knowledge of*
> *the LORD,*
> *just as the water covers the sea.*
>
> *(Isaiah 11:6-9)*

Micah joins Isaiah in offering this glimpse of the Kingdom:

> *They shall beat their swords into iron plows*
> *and their spears into pruning tools.*
> *Nation will not take up sword against nation,*
> *they will no longer learn how to make war.*
> *(Micah 4:3; Isaiah 2:4-5)*

The Bible's final book, the Book of Revelation, offers a compelling vision of what the kingdom of God will look like when it has fully come,

I saw a new heaven and a new earth, for the former heaven and the former earth had passed away, and the sea was no more. I saw the holy city, New Jerusalem, coming down out of heaven from God, made ready as a bride beautifully dressed for her husband. I heard a loud voice from the throne say, "Look! God's dwelling is here with humankind. He will dwell with them, and they will be his peoples. God himself will be with them as their God. He will wipe away every tear from their eyes. Death will be no more. There will be no mourning, crying, or pain anymore, for the former things have passed away." Then the one seated on the throne said, "Look! I'm making all things new."

(Revelation 21:1-5)

Scholars speak of these as "eschatological" images—the hoped-for completion and perfection of all things, the final state of our world. In each of these texts we see an end to violence, suffering, and pain. We see the world, not as it is, but as it was meant to be. Revelation describes a climax of history when, "The kingdom of the world has become the kingdom of our Lord and his Christ, and he will rule forever and always" (Revelation 11:15). Jesus came announcing that the kingdom of heaven has come near. He invited us to pray, "Thy kingdom come, thy will be done." But our prayer is not simply for the end of history as we know it, but that we might experience a taste of these things here and now. And not only that we will experience a foretaste of the final kingdom, but that we might be a part of bringing that kingdom near.

If we look around, we can see evidence of Thy kingdom come, Thy will be done, through people who have not only prayed but worked (*ora et labora*) to help our world look like this kingdom. Every summer, at an above-ground pool behind a house in what was one of the most violent neighborhoods in Kansas City, I have the joy of participating in a baptismal service organized by Bobbi Jo Reed. Bobbi Jo became an alcoholic at an early age. As a young woman she'd known homelessness and prostitution. She'd been assaulted and nearly killed. After a final stint in jail, she turned her life over to God. She prayed, "Thy kingdom come, thy will be done on earth as it is in heaven."

In 2002, Bobbi Jo had a vision to help other women like herself, women who would get out of jail, but had nowhere to land. These women would be back on the streets and back to their addiction, often a living hell. She took an inheritance she'd received at the death of one of her parents, and with it she purchased an abandoned nursing home in one of Kansas City's toughest neighborhoods. She fixed it up and started Healing House, providing transitional housing for women recovering from substance abuse (healinghousekc.org).

Soon there were more women seeking housing than room she had to offer. Bobbi Jo shared the vision with others, people who no doubt had also prayed, "Thy kingdom come, thy will be done." They helped purchase and renovate a second house, then a third and fourth and fifth, until today, there are houses and small apartment buildings scattered around Kansas City's historic northeast. There are 205 women, children, and men who now live in community at Healing House at any given time, and violent crime and crack houses have been virtually eliminated from this zip code.

Every summer at the above-ground pool, several dozen women, men, and children step into the pool, ask Jesus to wash them and make them new, and they are immersed, emerging from the water, often with tears, feeling born again, clean, and new. Thy kingdom come, Thy will be done, on earth as it is in heaven! God's kingdom is coming, God's will is being done, in and through Healing House.

Yet Christians also believe that there is a future, eschatological sense in which the Kingdom is yet to come, and will not fully come, until Christ ushers it in at the end of time. This is what Paul refers to in Philippians 3:20-21, "Our citizenship is in heaven. We look forward to a savior that comes from there—the Lord Jesus Christ. He will transform our humble bodies so that they are like his glorious body, by the power that also makes him able to subject all things to himself." So we pray for God's kingdom to come and God's will to be done, we long for and hope for this, and we offer ourselves to God that God might use us for this purpose. *And* we recognize that the kingdom of God will always be "already and not yet," among us and still to come, something we work to usher in, and something that can't fully be realized until Christ ushers it in at the last day.

The Will of God

As we pray, "thy will be done," it seems appropriate to pause to reflect upon God's will.

There are some who believe that everything happens according to God's will. In response to some disappointment, or some tragedy, they say in resignation, "It must have been the will of God." Or they might suggest in the face of suffering that, "Everything happens for a reason." If God is king of the universe, it is argued, God is sovereign and "in control," and therefore whatever happens must be the will of God.

While a verse here or there in Scripture might seem to support this view, a much larger body of biblical texts would point us to the fact that much of what happens in the world is not God's will. Believing God's sovereignty means, as many do, that whatever happens is God's will makes God ultimately responsible for the suffering and pain and tragedies that occur in the world. It also leads to a kind of fatalism that says, "Whatever will be will be. I can't change it. God will do what God wants to do. I resign myself to accepting my fate."

The very reason we must pray, "Thy kingdom come, thy will be done," is because God's will is often not done on earth as it is in heaven. We pray this precisely because God's sovereignty does not mean that everything that occurs happens because God wills it. We have to pray for God's kingdom to come and work for God's will to be done.

> # God's sovereignty does not mean that everything that occurs happens because God wills it.

Consider the ministry of Jesus. When Jesus walked this earth, he didn't approach the sick, the blind, the lame, the grieving, and say, "I'm so sorry, I can't help you because your illness, tragedy, or pain is the will of God." No! Instead, he assumes their condition is not God's will and he immediately works to rectify the situation.[3] We don't have the miraculous power that Jesus had, but we are meant to follow his example in being instruments of healing and help, love and care for people who are afflicted.

Bobbi Jo didn't assume that homelessness and addiction were God's will for the women on the streets. She assumed these were not God's will and she set about doing something to change things.

Suffering and tragedy are a part of life. Our bodies are susceptible to illness. And, as we'll see in chapter four, we sometimes hurt one another. In chapter five we'll pray for God to lead us away from temptation and evil, a prayer that is needed because we have a propensity to lead ourselves, like Adam and Eve, away from God's will, inflicting pain on ourselves and others. And our amazing planet has processes that are necessary to support life, which can also bring destruction. God isn't the cause of these things but walks with us through the adversity they bring. His will is to redeem these things and to force good from them.

James McGinnis has prayed the Lord's Prayer hundreds and hundreds of times across his twenty-five years of living. One evening during his senior year of high school, while playing football for his varsity team, he was severely injured, collapsing on the field. A subdural hematoma left him in the hospital for eighteen days. When he transferred to Madonna Rehabilitation Hospital in Nebraska, it was unclear if he would ever walk or talk again. Months later he came home and continued the long journey of learning how to walk and talk and feed himself.

Seven years later, he can walk, though with the gait of one who endured a severe head injury. He can talk, but slowly and carefully. His life was forever changed by this injury. But James and his parents, Patrick and Susan, have never believed that his injury was the will of God. They know this was an accident, the kind of traumatic brain injury that sometimes occurs in high school athletics.

I see James and his parents every weekend in worship. I deeply love this family. James is known in the church and by countless people in Kansas City for his infectious smile and his kind words. He's also known for constantly holding his hand up to make the American Sign Language sign for "I love you." This simple sign has become James's mission in life—to call people to love one another. He believes this is God's will for him. It is one way he can help God's kingdom to come and God's will to be done on earth as it is in heaven.

His father, Patrick, said to me, "We always tell people James's brain injury was not God's will. But we believe that adversity can build your faith, and reveal it, and that God can use it for good."

Wherever he goes, James scans the crowd to see who looks sad. As he approaches, he raises the "I love you" sign with his hand. Then he speaks, and as he does it is clear he's had some kind of traumatic injury that he has fought back from. Whoever he is speaking to is immediately won over. Walls come down. His smile, his outgoing spirit, and his love have a profound impact on people.

One night, while James and his parents were on a road trip, they stopped for gas. Soon a group of bikers pulled into the gas station to gas up as well. When it was time to pull away, James asked his dad to wait. James felt like he was supposed to go talk to the bikers. They looked a bit rough, and Patrick wasn't sure how these bikers would feel about James approaching. As James walked toward them, they did not appear friendly, but instead irritated by the interruption. James just smiled and flashed them the "I love you sign". Arms crossed, they did not smile back. But then they noticed James's gait, and when he spoke, they could tell that he'd had some kind of injury or disability. They were completely disarmed. He told them he felt he was supposed to stop to tell them that they were loved. One of the men broke down and began to cry, telling his story of growing up feeling rejected and unloved.

This is the impact James regularly has on people. In the midst of our polarized and conflicted society, James's presence and his love have brought Republicans and Democrats together. He's moved hardened people to compassion. He is a living, breathing sacrament of God's grace. Thy kingdom come, Thy will be done.

On Earth as It Is in Heaven

In their book on the Lord's Prayer, William Willimon and Stanley Hauerwas note a turning point in the prayer that comes at this phrase, "on earth as it is in heaven." They write, "Unexpectedly, quite surprisingly, politics has crept into our Christian praying at this point."[4] Here's why. We're not just praying "Thy kingdom come and Thy will be done" in our individual hearts and lives. Jesus teaches us to pray for God's kingdom to come and God's will to be done *on earth,* the way that it is in heaven. Every time we pray this prayer, we ask God for our planet to become what God intended for it to be. This is not just a personal and private vision. This is a vision for the world.

So when we pray this prayer, we are inviting God to give us a vision for the world as it should be—and then to not only pray, but to work to help that vision to become a reality.

When I speak on leadership, I often share a diagram I learned from Ron Heifetz who founded the Center for Public Leadership at Harvard's Kennedy School of Government. The diagram depicts a forty-five-degree angle made up of two arrows moving from left to right. The lower, horizontal arrow represents the world as it is. The arrow rising at an angle represents the word as it is supposed to be. Jesus described the world as it is supposed to be as the kingdom of God. Heifetz suggests that the role of leaders is to help people close the gap between the world as it is and the world as it is supposed to be. This is what we are praying for in the Lord's Prayer. Doing God's will and living this prayer involves closing the gap between the world as it is and the world as it is supposed to be.

Throughout 2020, I watched the political commercials, the rallies and debates at all levels of politics with a growing sense of frustration. Time and again, I saw both Republicans and Democrats, and the political action committees that fund many of their ads, completely misrepresent the truth about their political opponents, making them out to be scoundrels or idiots (or both). If you're running for office, I'm less interested in what's wrong with the other candidate and more interested in knowing what your vision is for a better world. What are the ways that you will work for the common good? If I vote for you, will the world look more like the kingdom of God than if I vote for your opponent? You shouldn't pray the Lord's Prayer during an election season without making the connection. Voting (and for some, running for office) is another way of seeking to live this part of our prayer.

I appreciate the way that New Testament scholar Frederick Dale Brunner rephrases this prayer so that we might hear its meaning in our modern culture. As he describes it, we are praying, "*Your* government come."[5] This is in essence what is meant by God's kingdom: God's rule, reign, and God's governing will.

The Lord's Prayer calls us to examine the world around us and ask, Where does the world as it is not align with the world as it should be?

The Lord's Prayer calls us to examine the world around us and ask, Where does the world as it is not align with the world as it should be? What would our world look like if God's will was done on earth as it is in heaven? Every public policy decision, every social issue, every place where humans suffer, is somehow meant to be affected by our praying and living the Lord's Prayer.

As we read our news feeds and watch the news, so many of the stories we see should drive us to our knees to pray this prayer, *Thy* kingdom come! *Thy* will be done, here on earth as it is in heaven. And then, in praying this prayer, we are driven back to our feet and out into the streets as agents of God's work to answer this prayer.

Racism and racial injustice: Thy kingdom come, Thy will be done! Global warming and environmental concerns: Thy kingdom come, Thy will be done! Poverty, food, and food insecurity: Thy kingdom come, Thy will be done!

By now you are beginning to see that the Lord's Prayer is more than a prayer; it is a vision to strive toward, a call to action we seek to live, and a road map for a life of character and faith. Each of us has our part to play in the coming of God's kingdom and the doing of God's will on earth as it is in heaven. And together, as churches, we can have a significant impact on "closing the gap" in our communities.

When I come to this line of Jesus's prayer, I ask myself, My or Thy? Mine or Thine? I think about the gap between earth and heaven. And I offer myself to Christ my king, inviting him to use me to close the gap so that God's kingdom may come and God's will be done in my life, in my community, and on earth as it is in heaven.

Would you join me in praying the prayer Jesus taught his disciples:

Our Father, who art in heaven, hallowed be thy *name.*
Thy kingdom come, thy will be done on earth as it is in heaven.
Give us this day our daily bread.
And forgive us our trespasses, as we forgive those who trespass against us.
And lead us, not into temptation, but deliver us from evil.
For thine *is the kingdom, and the power, and the glory, forever.*
Amen.

Our
Daily
Bread

3

Our Daily Bread

[Jesus said to them,] "After this manner therefore pray ye, Our Father which art in heaven, Hallowed be thy name.

Thy kingdom come, Thy will be done in earth, as it is in heaven.

Give us this day our daily bread."

(Matthew 6:9-11 KJV)

They asked [Jesus], "What miraculous sign will you do, that we can see and believe you? What will you do? Our ancestors ate manna in the wilderness, just as it is written, He gave them bread from heaven to eat*" . . . Jesus replied, "I am the bread of life. Whoever comes to me will never go hungry, and whoever believes in me will never be thirsty."*

(John 6:30-31, 35)

The Last Prayer We Pray

Jeff Hanson was one of the most remarkable human beings I've ever known. As a child he was diagnosed with neurofibromatosis type 1 (NF1) with an optic chiasmic brain tumor, leaving him visually impaired. He could not see what other kids could see. But as his parents discovered when he was twelve, he *could* see things other kids could not see. He loved to paint. He started with watercolor notecards, then moved on to acrylics on canvas. Within a few years this visually impaired artist became a phenomenon, with Elton John, Dale Earnhardt Jr., and Warren Buffet among the many who owned his works.

Jeff's story was told on *CBS Sunday Morning* and he was named a *People Magazine* "Hero Among Us." But at the age of twenty-seven, after years of keeping the neurofibromatosis at bay, Jeff began his last battle with the disease. I had been his pastor since he was a child. His family is an active and committed part of our congregation. I went to visit Jeff one last time shortly before his death. By this time he had not spoken for three days. His eyes were shut, but he would occasionally raise an eyebrow letting his parents and visitors know he was still with them.

As I sat with Jeff and his parents, we talked about Jeff's life and all of the amazing experiences he had had. Then we celebrated the ways he had impacted the world by his life, his art, and his generosity. We spoke about the hope we have in Christ as I read Scripture with the Hansons. Finally, I anointed Jeff's head with oil in the sign of the cross, and I took Jeff's hand as his mom and dad reached out to touch their son. We committed Jeff to God. We concluded our prayer with the Lord's Prayer, and as we did, for the first time in days, Jeff attempted to speak, mouthing the words to the prayer with us, "Our Father, who art in heaven..."

Within Judaism there is a set of words every practicing Jew learns to recite as a child. They are spoken daily by the faithful. These words are placed inside the mezuzah that is mounted to the doorpost of their homes. If you've seen a Jewish man or woman praying with a little black box on their forehead or arm, called *tefillin* or phylacteries, these are among the words found on the little scrolls within the *tefillin*. The words that are so important in Judaism are from Deuteronomy 6:4-5, and the passage is called the Shema, from the Hebrew word for "hear!" or "listen!" It begins:

> *Hear O Israel, the Lord is our God, the Lord is One.*

Then these words, added in the Second Temple period:

> *Blessed is the name of his Glorious Majesty forever and ever.*

Then the words Jesus called the first great commandment, as found in Deuteronomy 6:5:

> *You shall love the Lord your God with all your heart, with all your soul, and with all your might.*[1]

It is the hope of faithful Jews that these will be the last words on their lips at their death, and if they are unable to say them at that time, that someone will recite them on their behalf.

For many Christians, the closest thing we have to the Shema, in terms of something recited daily and at our death, is the Lord's Prayer. We know the great commandments Jesus named, but it is this prayer he taught us that often represents the final words on our lips, or on the lips of those who love us as they entrust us to God's safekeeping.

As we continue our study of the Lord's Prayer, having considered the first two lines, "Our Father, who art in heaven, hallowed be thy name. Thy kingdom come, thy will be done on earth as it is in heaven," we now turn to the third line, "Give us this day our daily bread." As with the first two sentences, we'll find there is much more here than we might at first suppose.

Give *Us* This Day *Our Daily* Bread

Let's begin by focusing on the little, seemingly insignificant word in this prayer—*daily*. It is found in the Greek of both Matthew's and Luke's version of the prayer. In Greek the word is *epiousian* (epee-ooh-see-on). I believe that this word is the key to making sense of this petition. But what makes this word particularly interesting is that it appears nowhere in the Greek language that we know of up to this point. It's appearance in Matthew and Luke is the earliest use of the word so far as we are aware. Remember, Jesus spoke in Aramaic, leaving early Christians to translate what he said into Greek, the universal language of the Roman Empire at the time. So, very early on in the history of Christianity, someone used *epiousian* to describe the bread Jesus was inviting us to pray for.

Epiousian doesn't literally translate as *daily*. In fact, we don't know exactly how to translate it. *Epi* means "on," "in," "upon," or "to." *Ousios* means "essence," "being," or "substance." So, *epiousian* would seem to mean "that which is needed for us to be" or "that which is essential." *Daily* doesn't fully capture the meaning of this Greek word (an issue that arises quite often when we translate ancient Greek, the language in which the New Testament was written, into modern English). "Our daily bread" might better be translated as "the essential bread," or "the bread we need to survive," or "the bread of subsistence." This petition in the prayer is better translated as: "Give us today the bread that we need to exist."

"Give us today the bread that we need to exist."

When I pray the Lord's Prayer, I do so as one who has food in the cupboard. I don't worry where my next meal will come from. But there are many who pray this prayer for whom this petition is, quite literally, a request for God to help them to have enough to eat. Let's focus for a moment on this prayer for physical bread and how God answers this prayer for those who are food insecure, struggling to meet the needs for the food required to feed their families.

According to the U.S. Department of Health and Human Services, the poverty level for a home with one person is just around $13,000. For a family of four it is around $26,000.[2] The U.S. Department of Agriculture reported that in 2019 more than one-third of Americans living below the poverty line were "food insecure," meaning they lack reliable access to an adequate supply of nutritious food.[3] In many of our schools, the majority of students come from households where the income is so low that they qualify for free or reduced-price lunches. These are communities where parents send their kids to bed at night without having enough to eat. Every single day, millions of our neighbors are praying, "Give us today the bread we need to survive."

In parts of Africa we find extreme, grinding poverty. One example is the small south central African nation of Malawi. Bounded by Tanzania to the north and east, Zambia to the west, and Mozambique to the south, Malawi is a beautiful land. But according to the International Monetary Fund, the average per capita income in Malawi in 2017 was $320 per year, making it among the poorest countries in the world. From 1995 to 2014, income levels rose by just 1.5 percent—not 1.5 percent per year, mind you, but just 1.5 percent *over a span of two entire decades.* Child malnutrition and the death of children under five worsened during this period.[4] In Malawi and other countries with extreme poverty, the people pray literally for the food they need to live.

How Does God Answer Prayers for Food?

Jesus taught us to pray "Give us this day our daily bread," but how should we expect God to answer our prayer? Unlike for the Israelites who found manna on the ground when they arose each day, God doesn't rain down food on our front lawn today. No, God's primary way of answering this prayer is, as we've learned of prayer in general, through people—people who pray "Thy kingdom come, thy will be done" and recognize in that prayer a call to action; people who pray those words and remember that in them they are praying, "Here I am, use me."

Those who have more than enough become the answer to the prayers of those who are lacking. We become the angels, the miracle workers, and the source of manna from God.

I remember feeling that so profoundly the first time I went to Malawi with a team from our church. We met with the tribal chiefs who told us of their most pressing concern: they longed for clean water sources so their children wouldn't get sick anymore. They had been praying to God for clean water, and then we showed up in their village asking how we could lend support to their visions for their people. To them, it seemed that we might be God's answer to their prayers. We felt the same and we began to look at what we could do to provide clean water for their people.

Likewise, sometime later, when flooding devastated many of their crops, and their seed had been destroyed, they prayed for daily bread. We heard God calling us to provide more seed and whatever else they would need to survive the disaster.

In Deuteronomy 15:10, God tells the Israelites: "Give generously to needy persons. Don't resent giving to them because it is this very thing that will lead to the Lord your God's blessing you in all you do and work at." When you read the longer passage in which this verse is found, a passage about the forgiveness of debts every seventh year, you may notice a couple of points. First, the call to give generously is not presented as a suggestion; it is given as a commandment. Second, here and elsewhere in Deuteronomy, God tells the Israelites (and us) that everything we have ultimately belongs not to us, but to God. And because it belongs to God, God can command us to give the poor some of the bounty "with which the Lord your God has blessed you" (Deuteronomy 15:14). Yet the willingness to obey the spirit of these commands, to be generous toward those in need, comes down to recognizing that God is *our* Father (Father to those who have and those who don't), our desire is to hallow God's name, and our prayer is for God's kingdom to come and God's will to be done.

This idea appears throughout Scripture. Proverbs 22:9 notes, "Those who are generous are blessed, for they share their bread with the poor" (NRSV). In Isaiah 58:6-7, God tells the Israelites about the kind of fasting he seeks from them during the days of their special religious observance: "Isn't this the fast I choose . . . sharing your bread with the hungry?"

Jesus may well have had this passage from Isaiah in mind as he taught his listeners that at the Last Judgment, those who refuse to help the poor will be excluded from the Kingdom, but those who helped and served the poor and those in need will be welcomed: "For I was hungry and you gave me food, I was thirsty and you gave me something to drink" (Matthew 25:35 NRSV).

Paul speaks of this in 2 Corinthians 8, when he asked the believers in Corinth to help with an offering for the Christians in Jerusalem who were poor and suffering: "At the present moment, your surplus can fill their deficit so that in the future their surplus can fill your deficit. In this way there is equality" (2 Corinthians 8:14). A few verses later Paul writes, "You will be made rich in every way so that you can be generous in every way" (2 Corinthians 9:11). In other words, we are blessed to be a blessing, just as God told Abraham (Genesis 12:1-4).

So, when we who have more than enough and pray, "Give us this day our daily bread," the emphasis should be on the *us* and *our*. "Give *us* this day *our* daily bread." I mentioned in the first chapter that Jesus teaches us to pray, "Our Father" not "My Father." In this petition we pray, "Give *us* this day *our* daily bread." We are praying for those who struggle, and, when we have more than enough, we are praying, "Use me and others so that all of us may eat."

Once more we see the idea of *ora et labora*, pray *and* work. This idea permeates Scripture and captures one part of what this petition might mean for us. James speaks about this as the need for both faith and works. I am reminded of James 2:15-17:

> *If a brother or sister is naked and lacks daily food, and one of you says to them, "Go in peace; keep warm and eat your fill," and yet you do not supply their bodily needs, what is the good of that? So faith by itself, if it has no works, is dead. (NRSV)*

I regularly remind our congregation that they answer this petition in the Lord's Prayer each Friday when they deliver 1,500 sacks filled with nutritious snacks to schools to be given to low-income children to help tide them over on the weekends (when they don't receive the free and reduced breakfast and lunches at school). They answer the prayer several times a year in our food drives distributing food to struggling families. They answer this prayer on Communion weekends when the special Communion offering is used to help people in the community who are unemployed or underemployed. They do it as they sponsor children through Compassion International and World Vision. They do it as they deliver produce to "food deserts" in Kansas City.

Jesus said, "To whom much has been given, much will be required" (Luke 12:48). He was echoing what we just read in Deuteronomy: Giving to the poor is not a helpful hint for living, but an essential rule in God's kingdom, the Kingdom we pray will come on earth as it is in heaven. But as we seek to meet the needs of others, we find that the blessing returns to us. As Francis of Assisi wrote, "It is in giving that we receive." It sounds countercultural in our materialistic society, but I have found that it is absolutely true: The happiest people I know are the people who are most generous. And some of the most spiritually and emotionally malnourished, impoverished, and unfulfilled people I know are people who have everything but share very little.

The Essential Food, the Food that We Need to Survive

Some pray for literal food. Others hear God's call to share with those in need. But daily bread in the prayer is more than the food we eat. This is clear, as we learned above, by Jesus's use of an adjective that Matthew and Luke record with the Greek word *epiousian*. While the word is often translated as "daily," it means something more like the food we need to exist or to be—our existential bread. Bread, then, is both what we eat, and what we need to exist or to be.

I cannot help but think about Maslow's "Hierarchy of Needs," an idea you may have learned about in high school psychology. Abraham Maslow first published the concept in 1943 as "A theory of Human Motivation." As it is popularly described, his theory posits that humans are motivated first by our most basic physical needs: air, food, water, and sex among them: our daily bread in the physical sense. But there are higher needs we have as well that include, in ascending order, safety and security, acceptance and love, self-esteem, including recognition and affirmation, and self-actualization or reaching our full potential. And, later in his life, Maslow would write of the desire for transcendence: living for a higher purpose, a life filled with meaning.

When Matthew and Luke use the Greek word *epiousian* to describe the bread Jesus told the disciples to pray for, the essential bread, the bread we need to exist, I think he was referring to these broader needs Maslow spoke about, the highest of which is the need for meaning and purpose and to connect with God.

There has been plenty of criticism of Maslow's idea, but at the very least it points to the full range of things we need as humans to survive. Give us this day our daily bread.

Throughout Scripture, bread is a metaphor for far more than food. I'm reminded of Jesus's words when the devil was tempting him to turn stones into bread. Jesus responded by quoting Deuteronomy (8:3), "One does not live by bread alone, / but by every word that comes from the mouth of God" (Matthew 4:4 NRSV).

In John, chapter four, when his disciples urge him to eat, Jesus says: "I have food to eat that you do not know about." Then, seeing their apparent confusion over his answer, he adds: "My food is to do the will of him who sent me and to complete his work" (John 4:32-34 NRSV). Once more, Jesus is pointing to something beyond bread that is essential to him, something that sustains him. It is meaningful work caring for others. Our food is to do the will of our Father, which is the very thing we pray just before praying for our daily bread, "thy will be done."

> **Our food is to do the will of our Father, which is the very thing we pray just before praying for our daily bread, "thy will be done."**

John 6 tells a story that begins with Jesus caring for others through acts of healing. He notices that a large crowd keeps following him, drawn to the "signs" of God's kingdom he was performing through these healing miracles. Jesus cares for them too. This crowd is hungry, so Jesus blesses the small quantity of bread and fish on hand and, miraculously, there is more than enough to feed five thousand people. He multiplies the fish and the loaves to feed the multitudes—it was real food for hungry people.

The next day, people from the crowd find Jesus again. They seem to be looking for another meal. Jesus says to them, "Do not work for the food that perishes, but for the food that endures for eternal life, which the son of Man will give you" (John 6:27 NRSV).

It is part of a remarkable exchange. Some in the crowd ask Jesus: "What miraculous sign will you do, that we can see and believe you? What will you do? Our ancestors ate manna in the wilderness, just as it is written, *He gave them bread from heaven to eat*" (6:30-31).

Jesus replies that the "true bread from heaven" came not from Moses, but from God. "The bread of God," he tells them, "is that which comes down from heaven and gives life to the world" (John 6:33). The people who came seeking a meal now are hungry for something more. "Sir," they say to Jesus, "give us this bread always" (v. 34).

Then Jesus says something most remarkable and, for many, perplexing: "I am the bread of life. Whoever comes to me will never go hungry, and whoever believes in me will never be thirsty" (v. 35).

This dramatic statement may hold the key to understanding the deeper meaning of our prayer for daily bread. In John's Gospel, we don't read about the Last Supper and the institution of the Eucharist or Holy Communion. Instead, it is in this story in chapter six that John points to the significance of the Eucharist. Here, after feeding the multitudes, Jesus teaches this profound truth: "I am the bread of life." John intends for his readers to think about the bread and wine of Holy Communion here.

At the Last Supper, Jesus took physical bread and wine and he offered them as a tangible means of receiving him: "The body of Christ, given for you," we hear as someone hands us the bread of the Eucharist. The bread is an expression of Christ's presence, and the life he wishes to give to us, to sustain us, strengthen us and nourish our souls. Will Willimon and Stanley Hauerwas, writing in *Lord, Teach Us*, got it right when they said, "When we want to meet God, we Christians do not go up some high mountain, do not rummage around in our psyches, do not hold hands, close our eyes and sing 'Kum Ba Yah'...We gather and break bread in Jesus' name. That's where he has chosen to meet us."[5]

When Jesus told us to pray for our *epiousion* bread—our essential, substantial bread, existential bread, the bread that sustains our souls, the bread we need to survive—he was inviting the hungry to pray for physical bread, inviting those who have enough to pray for those who don't and be moved to share, *and* he was teaching us to ask for and receive the bread that satisfies our soul. Jesus knew that we can have all the bread that we want, and yet be spiritually starved, just as we can have all the wealth that we could hope for, yet still be impoverished.

When I was assigned by Bishop W. T. Handy in 1990 to start the Church of the Resurrection, he sent me to start a church in the midst of a relatively affluent community in the southern part of the Kansas City metropolitan area. He was a large African American man whose booming voice sounded, to me, as I imagine the voice of God. He looked at me one day and said, "Son, don't let them fool you. There's a lot of poverty in the midst of those expensive houses. It's not a poverty of the pocketbook, but a poverty of the heart and soul." Give us this day our daily bread.

As an aside, notice that the next line of the Lord's Prayer begins with the word *And*. This is often left out when we pray, and even in some New Testament translations, but in the Greek, the word is clearly present. It is a conjunction, a word that is meant to link two ideas together. In the Lord's Prayer, "give us this day our daily bread" is linked to "forgive us our trespasses, as we forgive those who trespass against us." Among other things, the daily bread we ask for is God's forgiveness and mercy. Forgiveness is part of the essential bread we need to survive.

Forgiveness is part of the essential bread we need to survive.

When we're literally hungry and we can't do anything to help ourselves, we pray "Give us this day the bread that we need." When we have plenty and we pray "Give all of us this day the bread that we need," we are both praying for, and offering to help those in need. And we are also praying for the bread of life, for Christ who satisfies our hungry hearts. Give us this day, the bread that we need.

That takes me back to Jeff Hanson. At the age of twelve, while undergoing chemotherapy, Jeff started painting just to pass the time. One day he decided to open "Jeff's Bistro," a curbside bake sale, at the edge of his driveway to sell his mom's baked goods and his hand-painted note cards. He wanted to use part of the money he made to help other kids with tumors through the Children's Tumor Foundation.

People not only bought his note cards, but they thought they were really good. Soon, Jeff was encouraged to try his hand at painting on canvas using acrylics. The result was remarkable, and people began asking to buy his paintings.

The Make-a-Wish Foundation®, which grants wishes to critically ill children, granted a wish to Jeff. Jeff's wish was to meet Sir Elton John as he came to perform in concert in Kansas City. When Jeff met him backstage, the now fourteen-year-old artist presented Elton with a check for $1,000 for the Elton John Aids Foundation. This was part of the proceeds of his bistro and the sale of his art. He also gave Elton John one of his paintings. Elton was speechless. He'd agreed to meet with Jeff on his "Wish Night" to bless him. Instead, Jeff had just blessed and inspired Elton. This was the beginning of a friendship that continued for the rest of Jeff's life.

This focus on helping others and using his art to raise money for causes he cared about became Jeff's passion. With each passing year, his art matured and more and more people were clamoring for it. He began donating some of his art to charity. Soon, people were paying thousands of dollars for his work. As a teen, Jeff set a goal of giving one million dollars to charity through his art by the time he reached his twentieth birthday, a goal he accomplished. Part of what he discovered, and one of the pillars of his life, was that "generosity begets generosity." His generosity led others to be more generous.

At the age of twenty he set a new goal. He hoped to give away ten million dollars to organizations focused on helping people by the time he was thirty. He found such joy in helping others. Jeff articulated a guiding principle in his life as,

> Every act of kindness helps create kinder communities, more compassionate nations and a better world for all...even one painting at a time.

Jeff lived the Lord's Prayer. He did not believe God gave him NF1, but he did believe God was using it, and him, to help others. Jeff provided daily bread to others through the gifts of his art and the donations he made, and in the process, found the *epiousian* bread of meaning and purpose, love and joy that fed his own soul.

Jeff didn't live to be thirty; had he lived that long I have no doubt he would have hit his goal of ten million dollars donated to charity. But before he died at the age of twenty-seven he had sold 2,475 paintings, 100,967 notecards, and generated $7.2 million for over 200 charities.[6]

In the end, the last words Jeff would ever speak were the words of the Lord's Prayer. Let's pray them together…

> *Our Father, who art in heaven, hallowed be thy name.*
> *Thy kingdom come, thy will be done on earth as it is in heaven.*
> *Give* us *this day* our *daily bread.*
> *And forgive us our trespasses, as we forgive those who trespass against us.*
> *And lead us, not into temptation, but deliver us from evil.*
> *For* thine *is the kingdom, and the power, and the glory, forever.*
> *Amen.*

4

FORGIVE . . .
AS WE
FORGIVE

4
FORGIVE...
AS WE FORGIVE

"After this manner therefore pray ye: Our Father which art in heaven, Hallowed be thy name.

Thy kingdom come, Thy will be done in earth, as it is in heaven.

Give us this day our daily bread.

And forgive us our debts, as we forgive our debtors . . .

For if ye forgive [others] their trespasses, your heavenly Father will also forgive you:

But if ye do not forgive [others] their trespasses, neither will your Father forgive your trespasses."

(Matthew 6:9-12, 14-15 KJV)

They also led two other criminals to be executed with Jesus. When they arrived at the place called The Skull, they crucified him, along with the criminals, one on his right and the other on his left. Jesus said, "Father, forgive them, for they don't know what they're doing."

(Luke 23:32-34)

Recently I was reading stories of parents teaching their children the Lord's Prayer. Sometimes what the children heard, as they were learning the prayer, wasn't what their parents intended to teach. A three-year-old named Reese recited the prayer in this way: "Our Father, who does art in heaven, Harold is his name. Amen." A four-year-old prayed, "And forgive us our trash baskets as we forgive those who put trash in our baskets."[1]

One woman wrote that she had been teaching her three-year old daughter, Caitlin, the Lord's Prayer for several evenings at bedtime. The little girl would repeat it every night, line by line, after her mother. When she felt she could do it on her own, Caitlin prayed, "Lead us not into temptation, but deliver us some E-mail. Amen."[2]

Sometimes even adults fail to understand the meaning and power of what we are praying in the Lord's Prayer.

As we turn to the next petition Jesus calls us to pray, we once again come to an essential part of the gospel of Jesus: forgiveness and reconciliation. It would be difficult to overstate its importance in the ministry of Jesus, for our world, and in our lives. Without forgiveness our world is left with vengeance and retribution. In our spiritual life, without forgiveness we're left with a life of guilt and alienation from God. Without forgiveness in our interpersonal lives, no marriage can survive, no friendship will endure, and humanity is condemned to bitterness, resentment, anger, and hate. Researchers have linked unforgiveness to higher stress, poorer mental health, and cardiac diseases.[3]

This simple line, "Forgive us our trespasses as we forgive those who trespass against us," is not only central to the gospel, it is central to life. The two sides of this prayer, "forgive us" and "as we forgive," capture this essential idea: We all need forgiveness, and we must extend forgiveness. Every time we pray this prayer, we are both seeking and being reminded to extend forgiveness. Once again we can see why the author of the *Didache* called early Christians to pray the Lord's Prayer three times a day.

What Is Forgiveness?

Let's start by attempting to define *forgiveness*. It's a word we all think we know and understand, but it's helpful to clarify what we do and don't mean by the word. Let's begin with the Greek word for *forgive* used in the Lord's Prayer: *aphiemi*. It means to let go, to release, or to send away. Forgiveness is letting go, releasing, sending away the resentment or the right to exact revenge. We're asking God to release us from God's right to hold our sins over us, to release us from the guilt and shame we feel.

That doesn't mean that all the consequences of our sin have been released. If our sin involves wronging another, breaking a law, or otherwise has had some impact upon others or the world, we're usually going to need to do what we can do to make things right by addressing the impact our sin had on others. There may be legal consequences to our actions.

Likewise, when we forgive others we are choosing to let go of our right to vengeance, or retribution, our right to hate the one who trespassed against us or the right to hold the grievance over their heads. It does not excuse the action of the one who wronged us. It does not say that it didn't matter. Forgiveness is also not reconciliation with the other, though reconciliation sometimes occurs after forgiveness. And as is true with our own sins, sometimes there are ongoing consequences to another's actions even if you forgive them. They may still be required to make restitution, for instance, or they may never be someone you place in a position of trust again. Forgiveness is not forgetting, but forgiveness is releasing our resentment, our visions of retribution, our bitterness and hate.

Forgiveness is both a choice and a process. This is true in accepting it for yourself, as well as in practicing it toward others. And in the Lord's Prayer and elsewhere in the Gospels, Jesus links God's forgiveness with our forgiveness of others. In a sense we cannot fully accept God's forgiveness when we continue to hold on to our anger or bitterness toward others.

A Bag of Rocks

As a pastor, on many occasions I've heard the confessions of those struggling with guilt. I've also ministered with people who bore resentment toward those who had wronged them, who became increasingly bitter and angry with these emotions slowly eating away at their souls. Some years ago, I wrote a little book on forgiveness as an attempt to help others to forgive.[4]

In the book and in sermons I've preached on forgiveness, I use a metaphor others have found helpful to illustrate the weight of our sins and, conversely, the weight of bitterness and resentment when we refuse to forgive others.

As I preach on this subject, I'll have a table before me with a large pile of rocks of varying sizes. And I'll have a backpack into which I'll place the rocks. I begin by talking about the sins we commit, those things we've done to sin against God and others. I'll grab a couple of handfuls of small stones representing the small sins we commit, and I'll place them in the backpack as I talk about the little white lies, the moments of anger or irritation, the thoughts, words, and deeds that are lesser offenses, but still real. Next, I grab handfuls of the midsized rocks representing the more egregious sins we've committed against God and others, and I stuff them into the backpack. Finally, I grab several of the really large rocks and describe the more serious sins we commit, and the weight of guilt and shame we feel after committing these. I toss them in the backpack, zip it up, and start carrying it on my back, a thirty- to forty-pound burden. I continue the sermon talking about the weight of sin and guilt and shame and how these can sap the energy and joy from us.

After about ten minutes of this, the congregation can see me visibly beginning to struggle, eventually becoming a bit short of breath. This becomes a picture of what happens in each of our lives as we try to carry our guilt and shame rather than seeking forgiveness from God and others. The very fact that Jesus told us we should ask for forgiveness reveals two things: first, we all sin and need forgiveness, and second, God is willing to forgive us. At this point, I speak about repentance—the act of acknowledging the wrong, expressing the remorse we feel, and we commit to doing our best not to repeat the acts. It is then that I let the bag drop with a thud.

The congregation can see the release on my face, hear it in how I am speaking and breathing, and see it in the sudden strength and joy I feel, finally free of my sins. Forgive us our trespasses!

Subsequently, I consider the other side of the petition Jesus teaches us to pray in the Lord's Prayer: "as we forgive those who trespass against us." Once again I use the illustration, with the same rocks on the table and the same backpack, but now these rocks represent the small, medium, and large sins others commit against us. With each category of stones, I demonstrate what it looks like to hold on to our bitterness and resentment by stuffing them into the backpack, again, giving examples of each type of grievance or offense committed against us. I zip up the backpack with its thirty to forty pounds of "grievances," and this time I strap the backpack to my chest, indicating my unwillingness to forgive, holding on to my resentment, and the hardening of my heart. The backpack also serves as a visible reminder of how resentment separates me and my heart from God and others. As I continue with the sermon, the congregation can, once again, see me becoming winded, and I start to hunch over a bit while I'm preaching

Finally, I talk about the power and importance of forgiveness—of letting go. We talk about what forgiveness is not: it is not excusing the offense. It is not saying it didn't matter. It is not saying it is okay. It is not forgetting or reconciliation or a restored relationship. Forgiveness is choosing to let go or release the right to retribution, anger, or bitterness. It is letting go of the right to hold the offense over another's head. Now I drop the bag again and it once more lands with a thud. I can stand up straight again. I can talk without being winded. I feel a lightness as I walk that is amazing after carrying that pack around for a while. That is what forgiveness feels like. Forgive us our trespasses *as we forgive those who trespass against us!*

Forgiveness is choosing to let go or release the right to retribution, anger, or bitterness. It is letting go of the right to hold the offense over another's head.

Both receiving and granting forgiveness are represented in the words Jesus teaches us to pray. Every time we pray this prayer, we are both asking for forgiveness and hearing Christ's call to forgive.

Our Need and God's Gift

So much of Jesus's life and ministry was devoted to teaching, and offering, forgiveness. He was constantly reaching out to people who were estranged from God and seeking to woo them back to his Father. In the parable of the prodigal son, he taught that God was like a father whose younger son ran off and squandered all he had on wild living. But when the son returned, penitent, his father wrapped his arms around the boy, and welcomed him. The father had been waiting and longing for his child to come home. That, Jesus said, is what God is like.

I mentioned the parable of the Pharisee and the tax collector in the Introduction. Listen to Jesus's words:

> "Two people went up to the temple to pray. One was a Pharisee and the other a tax collector. The Pharisee stood and prayed about himself with these words, 'God, I thank you that I'm not like everyone else—crooks, evildoers, adulterers—or even like this tax collector. I fast twice a week. I give a tenth of everything I receive.' But the tax collector stood at a distance. He wouldn't even lift his eyes to look toward heaven. Rather, he struck his chest and said, 'God, show mercy to me, a sinner.' I tell you, this person went down to his home justified rather than the Pharisee."
>
> (Luke 18:10-14)

The tax collector went away justified, not because of his righteous acts, but because of his humble expression of penitence and his longing for God's mercy. "Forgive us our sins."

Jesus showed mercy to the woman caught in the act of adultery in John 8. He called both Levi and Zacchaeus, two tax collectors considered particularly sinful, to follow him. He forgave a man literally paralyzed by guilt. And the "sinful woman"—most likely a prostitute—in Luke 7 was freely forgiven. There was the Samaritan woman who was married and divorced five times, to whom Jesus offered "living water."

At the end of his life, Jesus sat with his disciples at a meal of bread and wine. He took the bread and gave thanks, broke it, and gave it to his disciples saying, "This is my body, which is broken for you" (1 Corinthians 11:24 KJV). And after the supper was over he took the cup and said, "This is my blood of the covenant poured out for many *for the forgiveness of sins*" (Matthew 26:28 NIV, italics added). And from the cross, he looked down upon those who had nailed him there and prayed, for them and for us, "Father, forgive them, for they don't know what they're doing" (Luke 23:34).

I recount all of this to say that the fourth petition of the Lord's Prayer captures what was such a huge part of Jesus's message and ministry. Which tells us that when he invites us to pray for God's forgiveness, and we express penitence, we can have assurance that God not only hears us but forgives us. "Forgive us our trespasses, as we forgive those who trespass against us."

Forgive Us Our *Sins*

In Luke's account of the Lord's Prayer, Jesus teaches his disciples to pray, "Forgive us our sins." In Matthew's account Jesus taught them to pray, "Forgive us our debts." Most English-speaking Protestants, Catholics, and Orthodox pray, "Forgive us our trespasses." But many pray, "Forgive us our debts." Which is it, sins, debts, or trespasses? Let's spend a bit of time with this question as a way of deepening our understanding of this part of our prayer.

In Luke's version, Jesus teaches his disciples to pray, "Forgive us our sins, for we ourselves forgive everyone indebted to us" (Luke 11:4 NRSV). The Greek word for "sin" is *hamartia*. It is an archery term that meant to miss the target. You string your arrow, pull it back, and let go, but the arrow falls short of the target, or overshoots it, or the arrow flies to the right or left—the word is *hamartia*. But by the New Testament period, *hamartia* was the primary word for "sin."

The metaphor is rich and meaningful. In life, there is a target for how we're meant to live. Scripture is filled with verses trying to describe the target. This includes the great commandments to love God with our entire being and to love our neighbor as we love ourselves. Scripture calls us to do justice, love mercy, and walk humbly with God. It calls us to "do unto others as you would have them do unto you." We're called to follow Jesus, to "not be overcome by evil but to overcome evil with good," to "live a life worthy of the calling," and to exhibit the "fruit of the Spirit." You get the idea. While we may know all of these Scriptures pointing toward the target or mark we're meant to pursue, none of us perfectly lives them; we all miss the target—*hamartia*.

When we look at Scripture closely, we find that all of the Bible's heroes were fallible human beings, yet God forgave them, walked with them, loved them, and used them. The Bible's patriarchs, Abraham, Isaac, and Jacob, were each, in their own ways, a mess. Sarah was cruel to Hagar. Moses killed a man. King David may have composed or commissioned many of our psalms, but at his worst moment, recorded in Scripture for us to read, he was an adulterer and had a man killed to cover up his sin. Esther at first lacked courage. Joseph was ready to divorce Mary. Peter denied knowing Jesus. The rest of the apostles abandoned Jesus. Judas betrayed him. Paul participated in the stoning of Stephen before he came to faith. I take great comfort in seeing the flawed saints throughout Scripture. Why are we allowed to see their shortcomings? In part, I believe, to help us see that God chooses flawed people, forgives them, befriends them, and uses them. What other choice does God have?

With some regularity, I have to remind myself of God's willingness to forgive. I have an ideal (my wife would say, unrealistic) picture of what it means to be a faithful follower of Jesus and a pastor. I would never hold others to these expectations, and I can never fully live up to them. It is this that leads me to love this line in our prayer inviting us to pray for God's forgiveness. Forgive us our *sins*.

Forgive Us Our Debts

Throughout this book we've been using the version of this prayer customarily used by Catholics, Orthodox, and many Protestants in the English-speaking world, "Forgive us our trespasses, as we forgive those who trespass against us." Above we saw that Luke has a different version: "Forgive us our sins, for we ourselves forgive everyone indebted to us." But nearly every English translation of the prayer from Matthew has, "And forgive us our debts, as we also have forgiven our debtors." Which is it, debts or trespasses?

Jesus teaches us to pray, forgive us our *opheilemata*. It literally refers to something owed to another. Hence, the better translation of Matthew's account of the Lord's Prayer is "forgive us our debts as we forgive our debtors." In the time of Jesus, everyone understood the metaphor of debt as it related to sin and forgiveness. Jesus spoke frequently in his teaching and parables about debts. Most common people—and that was most of the population of Galilee and Judea during the time of Jesus—owed someone something at some point during the year. The tenant farmers were living on leased land and may have borrowed money for seed. To repay their debt, they gave a portion of their crops to the landlord and lenders at harvest time. If the harvest was poor, their debt carried over into the next crop season. Without regular paychecks, and with droughts and taxes and other obligations, it was not uncommon for working people to owe something to someone multiple times each year. They might never be free of their debts.

When someone got so far in debt that they could never possibly repay, the creditor might show mercy for a time. An extravagantly kind and merciful person might completely and permanently forgive the debt. But typically, there were two fates in the Greco-Roman world for people indebted in a way that they could not repay: They either became a slave until they worked off the debt, or they languished in debtor's prison until someone paid off the debt for them. The act of paying off another person's debt was called *redemption*, and the person who did this was called a *redeemer*.

The use of the word *debt* in the Lord's Prayer was a powerful metaphor, as all of Jesus's hearers knew what happened to debtors who could not repay. Jesus taught his disciples to ask for God to cancel their debts. When it comes to the debts that need to be forgiven, the idea involves what is owed to God. Our sins of omission are debts in the form of good deeds God expected that we did not fulfill. Our sins of commission are debts we've incurred by wrongdoing for which we must atone or make amends with God.

If you've ever walked through a store of fragile things, you may have seen a sign that says, "You break it, you buy it." It is a reminder that you are responsible for what you cause to happen, whether intentionally or accidentally, and you'll be required to pay. The idea of debts related to our sins is similar. Paul uses a slightly different metaphor when he speaks of the "wages of sin." There is a debt incurred by sin. Matthew's use of this word is a metaphor meant to recognize the burden of our sins, and the generosity of God in releasing us from our debts. Likewise, we're meant to be willing to forgive the debts of others, releasing the debt of those who have sinned against us.

We're meant to be willing to forgive the debts of others, releasing the debt of those who have sinned against us.

Both in Acts and in Paul's epistles, this metaphor of debts and being redeemed from our debts is used. In Galatians 4 we read, "God sent his Son, born through a woman, and born under the Law. This was so he could redeem those under the Law" (vv. 4-5). You've likely heard the line from the old gospel song, "He paid a debt he did not owe. I owed a debt I could not pay." Forgive us our debts!

Jesus captures both the idea of our debt being paid or canceled, and the need for us in turn, to forgive the debts of others, in a powerful parable in Matthew 18:23-35. A man was about to be sold into slavery, along with his entire family, because he owed the king a vast sum of money. But the man pleaded with the king for mercy. In an extraordinary gesture, the king goes beyond giving the man more time to repay the debt; he simply cancels the entire debt. He writes off a fortune and sets the man and his family free. That is a picture of what God does for us, with Jesus paying our debts with his life.

But how does the man respond to this extravagant, amazing act of grace? On his way out of the king's palace, he happens to encounter someone who owes him a relatively small amount of money compared to his own debt to the king. Instead of extending the mercy that he has just received, he demands payment in full and threatens to have the luckless fellow thrown in jail. When the king hears of it, he reinstates the debt of the ungrateful servant and imprisons him. This is the very idea Jesus includes in the Lord's Prayer when he asks us to pray, Forgive our debts, *as we forgive our debtors.*

To Jesus's first-century hearers, most of whom owed debt and knew the consequences of nonpayment, thinking of their sins as debts and others who sinned against them as debtors was powerful and illuminating. To see their obligations toward God, and sins against God, in terms of debt highlighted their need for redemption and God's grace in redeeming them.

The prayer also points to Christ's call to similarly release the debts of others. This certainly meant forgiving the sins of others; but as we saw in the last chapter, in Deuteronomy 15, God makes a remarkable demand that his people forgive actual debts every seven years. While Jesus makes clear in Matthew 6:14-15 that the debt he's referring to is wrongs done to us, some wonder if his use of the term is also meant to lead us to practice economic forgiveness when we are owed money by someone who is struggling to repay. I say this not because it is a requirement of this passage, but as something suggested by this passage and required of the ancient Israelites in Deuteronomy. On several occasions I've had people who owed me money, but for whom the repayment was a hardship, and I've forgiven the debt knowing all that I have belongs to God and inspired by how much God has forgiven my debts. Forgive us our debts, as we forgive our debtors.

Forgive Us Our Trespasses

Understanding the significance of debt, let's turn to the meaning of *trespasses* and why this word was used by William Tyndale in his 1526 English translations of the New Testament and is still used by large numbers of English-speaking people today.

In the two verses that follow the Lord's Prayer, Jesus comments and expands upon the line of the prayer we've been studying in this chapter, saying, "For if you forgive others their trespasses, your heavenly Father will also forgive you; but if you do not forgive others, neither will your Father forgive your trespasses" (Matthew 6:14-15 NRSV). Notice that Jesus uses the word *trespasses* here, twice, as he reiterates what he has said already in the prayer, "Forgive us our debts as we forgive our debtors."

The Greek word that we translate into English as "trespass" is *paraptōmata*, which literally means falling away or a misstep, perhaps intentional but often unintentional. When we see "no trespassing" signs we understand we are not to step onto the property. If we go on to step on another's property against their will, when we trespass, we violate another person's property, space, or will. Imagine coming home to find a complete stranger had entered your unlocked door, uninvited, rummaging through your things. They would be trespassing, and you would feel violated.

By definition, trespassing is going on a path you are not meant to embark on—and in this way it is a similar metaphor to the archer's term, *hamartia*—to miss the target. Thus the Common English Bible actually translates *paraptōmata* not as "trespass" but as "sin."

In the end, debts, trespasses, and sins all intend to speak to our violation of others and of God. In my relationship with God, I have incurred debts, I have missed the mark, and I have trespassed, treading where I am not meant to tread or violating another's rights. Forgive us our trespasses, forgive us our debts, or forgive us our sins—in a sense, they are three different ways of saying the same thing.

As We Forgive Those Who Trespass Against Us

We've noted this petition is both about asking for God's forgiveness and Christ's call for us to forgive others. But it's time to take a closer look at the second half of this petition. Jesus doesn't just tell us to pray for God to forgive us, and that we should forgive others. He tells us to pray, "Forgive us our debts, *as we also have forgiven* our debtors." Said another way, "Forgive us our wrongs in the same way and to the same degree as we forgive those who wrong us." He has us directly link the grace we ask for to the grace we are willing to show toward others. Yikes!

I believe the linkage between God's forgiveness and our willingness to forgive is twofold. It is hard to accept God's forgiveness when you are unforgiving toward others. How can you trust in God's mercy when you live unmercifully? And second, when we've yet to learn mercy, and we continue to hold on to bitterness, resentment, and anger, it seems odd that we would ask God for the very thing we're unwilling to give to others. But growing in grace toward others opens our hearts to accepting God's grace for ourselves.

But is it really true that God will only forgive us if we forgive others? There are forms of hurt others inflict upon us that may take years to work through before we can let go of the resentment. Will God not forgive our sins until then? Here's what I think: Jesus often speaks in what is sometimes called "prophetic hyperbole." To speak prophetically is to speak in broad, black-and-white terms without trying to address exceptions to the rule. To speak in hyperbole is to use exaggeration to make a point. Jesus often makes bold, sweeping statements to make a point, but we interpret these in the light of his ministry with people, where we find an abundance of grace.

"If your right eye causes you to sin, tear it out" (Matthew 5:29 NRSV) is a great example. He is not actually advocating that we tear out our eyes or cut off our hands (another part of this statement in Matthew). He is speaking in a way that shakes us up and makes his point that sin is serious. He says, "It's easier for a camel to squeeze through the eye of a needle than for a rich person to enter God's kingdom." I love the reaction of the disciples to this last statement: they were stunned and they asked, "Then who can be saved?" Then, "Jesus looked at them carefully and said, 'It's impossible for human beings. But all things are possible for God'" (Matthew 19:24-26). I wonder if Jesus's words about God's unwillingness to forgive us when we don't forgive others are a bit like these examples. God surely understands how hard forgiveness can be at times. But his words here, I believe, are less about a hard and fast rule regarding his unwillingness to forgive than they are about *our* need to forgive others. And he knew that human society cannot survive without humans exercising grace toward one another.

Jesus routinely taught his disciples to forgive. In addition to what we've read in Matthew 6:14-15 and what Jesus mentions in the Lord's Prayer, Mark 11:25 records, "Whenever you stand up to pray, if you have something against anyone, forgive so that your Father in heaven may forgive you your wrongdoings." (This is as close as Mark comes to including the Lord's Prayer in his Gospel.) In Luke 6:37 Jesus says, "Forgive, and you will be forgiven." In Luke 17:3-5, Jesus offers a word about prayer that seems too difficult to his disciples:

"If your brother or sister sins, warn them to stop. If they change their hearts and lives, forgive them. Even if someone sins against

you seven times in one day and returns to you seven times and says, 'I am changing my ways,' you must forgive that person."

The apostles said to the Lord, 'Increase our faith!'"

In Matthew 18, in what may be a parallel passage to the one above in Luke, Jesus instructs the disciples to approach a fellow believer who is sinning in order to call them to stop. And if they stop, they are to forgive them. Then Peter says to Jesus, "Lord, how many times should I forgive my brother or sister who sins against me? Should I forgive as many as seven times?" Jesus said, "Not just seven times, but rather as many as seventy-seven times" (Matthew 18:21-22).

Note that in both of these passages, forgiveness was tied to the one who had sinned repenting—changing their ways. If someone repents, has a change of mind, heart, and behavior, you keep forgiving, even if they continue to struggle. Here I'd remind you that forgiveness is not the same as excusing behavior or eliminating consequences. I've known people, usually women, in abusive marriages. The abuser feels terrible after each episode and promises to change yet continues to abuse. Forgiveness is not returning to an abusive marriage. It is letting go of the bitterness, anger, and desire for retribution. Matthew 18 and Luke 17 are not requiring that you return to an abuser, or trust a cheater, or eliminate all consequences for harmful behavior—which may actually enable and harm the person you are forgiving.

Robin Casarjian, author of a book called *Forgiveness: A Bold Choice for a Peaceful Heart*, writes that "Forgiveness is…a favor we do for ourselves…in order to free ourselves."[5] A study published in 2012 in the *Journal of Behavioral Medicine* found that letting go of the right to "revenge, resentment, or harsh judgments" toward one who caused hurt, without any conditions attached, increased longevity and health.[6] We allow those who inflict harm to keep harming us to the degree that we continue to hold on to our resentment over long periods of time. They continue to have control over us.

But aside from the really big rocks—the terribly painful hurts inflicted on us—forgiveness is most often about navigating everyday life. People will hurt us. They will disappoint us. Some will not see things from our perspective. We either carry the rocks with us, or we release them (remember, *aphiemi* = forgive = release).

LaVon and I will be celebrating our fortieth wedding anniversary within a few months of this book's release. We married the week after high school graduation. Can I tell you how many small and medium-sized rocks we'd be carrying around in our backpack over these forty years if we did not forgive? Every week one of us will snap at the other about something, or we'll take a tone of voice, or find ourselves irritated about something. It seldom lasts long before one of us says, "I am sorry," and the other says, "I forgive you."

In every friendship there are moments of disappointment, hurt, or betrayal. There can be no friendship without forgiveness. The same is true in the workplace, at school, and even at church. We cannot sustain any long-term relationships without forgiveness, the willingness to let go. Forgiveness, not anger, bitterness, and retribution, are what the kingdom of God looks like. Are there people you need to forgive today? People you need to release from the right to hold something over their head?

We cannot sustain any long-term relationships without forgiveness, the willingness to let go.

I interrupted my work on this chapter to visit with a woman in our congregation. She was sharing with me the story of her aunt, a deeply devout Christian. But she described for me the way her aunt never seemed to forget some offenses committed by other family members. It wasn't so much that she carried resentment, but she had a way of regularly bringing back up these offenses from the past. She did so as if she were joking, but those who had committed the offenses, who had sought forgiveness long before, continued to feel her holding these things over them by the regular repetition of these things. Her aunt would have said that she forgave all who had wronged her, but she continued to recite the wrongs in a way that left others feeling unforgiven. She failed to understand that forgiving involves releasing.

The Really, Really Big Stones

I recently met Dr. Izzeldin Abuelaish. He was speaking at an annual event focused on kindness called SevenDays, started by

Resurrection member Mindy Corporon after the murder of her father and son.[7] Mindy has devoted a significant part of her life to working for kindness and, in the words of the apostle Paul, not being overcome by evil, but overcoming evil with good. Each year she invites guest speakers to Kansas City, people who have demonstrated a remarkable willingness to let go of terrible wrongs done to them.

Dr. Abuelaish was born and raised in the Jabalia refugee camp in Gaza. He received his medical doctorate at the University of Cairo and earned a diploma in Obstetrics and Gynecology from the University of London. He completed his residency at Soroka Medical Center in Israel and earned a master's degree in public health from Harvard. He was the first Palestinian to practice medicine on staff at an Israeli hospital, delivering hundreds of babies, both Israelis and Palestinians.

On January 16, 2009, an Israeli tank fired two mortar shells into his home in Gaza. Three of his daughters were killed along with his niece. He was serving as a correspondent for an Israeli news station at the time, and as he walked through his home, in shock and disbelief, he called his friends at the station, interrupting the nightly newscast begging them to get ambulances to his home. The incident was recorded live on the evening news as he cried out in shock and overwhelming sorrow.

Such an event might have provoked hatred and a desire for vengeance. This is the cycle that occurs frequently in Israel and Palestine. Instead, Dr. Abuelaish chose to focus the rest of his life on working for peace. I sat in awe listening to him, twelve years later, describe his pain, and then his determination to forgive. He said, "We cannot allow tragedy and death and pain to be the end of our lives. I want to honor my daughters by turning this tragedy into a blessing. We must work for justice, but with what? A bullet? That is the instrument of the weak. No, with kindness we will work for justice and for peace."

His ability to endure such pain, and to work for peace, to demonstrate kindness in the face of a terrible injustice, is precisely what makes his words and his work so compelling. You can read his story in his remarkable memoir, *I Shall Not Hate: A Gaza Doctor's Journey on the Road to Peace and Human Dignity.* Though he is Muslim, in so many ways he is more Christian than many Christians that I know. Forgive us our trespasses, as we forgive those who trespass against us.

In a sermon called "To Whom Much Is Forgiven," twentieth-century theologian and philosopher Paul Tillich once said, "Forgiveness is an answer, the divine answer, to the question implied in our existence."[8] It is part of the daily bread we need, and which we must be willing to extend.

This fourth line of the prayer Jesus taught us holds the key to finding life not only for ourselves, but also for the survival of our broken world. Paul reminds us, "Do not be overcome by evil, but overcome evil with good" (Romans 12:21 NRSV). Jesus commands us, "Love your enemies and pray for those who harass you" (Matthew 5:44). And we're meant to pray daily, "Forgive us our trespasses, as we forgive those who trespass against us."

With all of this in mind, let's once again pray the prayer that Jesus taught us to pray,

Our Father, who art in heaven, hallowed be thy name.
Thy kingdom come, thy will be done on earth as it is in heaven.
Give us this day our daily bread.
And forgive us our trespasses, as we forgive those who trespass against us.
And lead us, not into temptation, but deliver us from evil.
For thine is the kingdom, and the power, and the glory, forever.
Amen.

5

AND LEAD US, NOT INTO TEMPTATION...

5

And Lead Us, Not into Temptation...

And don't lead us into temptation,
but rescue us from the evil one.
(Matthew 6:13)

He leadeth me in the paths of righteousness for his name's sake.
(Psalm 23:3 KJV)

No one, when tempted, should say, "I am being tempted by
God";

for God cannot be tempted by evil and he himself tempts no one.
But one is tempted by one's own desire, being lured and enticed
by it; then, when that desire has conceived, it gives birth to sin,
and that sin, when it is fully grown, gives birth to death.
(James 1:13-15 NRSV)

Like a roaring lion your adversary the devil prowls around look-
ing for someone to devour. Resist him, steadfast in your faith.
(1 Peter 5:8-9 NRSV)

During a retreat, four Christian men were getting really honest with each other about their struggles in life. One man said, "My biggest temptation is lust. I'm embarrassed to admit it." The next guy said, "My struggle is gambling. No one knows this, but I occasionally am tempted to sneak off to the casinos." A third guy chimed in, "My temptation is alcohol, and I've often drunk way more than I should." The last man said, "Guys, I hate to tell you this, but my greatest temptation is gossip. And if you'll excuse me, I need to post a few things to social media."[1]

I wonder what temptation looks like for you?

In writing this book I've come to realize just how often I pray the Lord's Prayer, personally and in ministry settings. The week I was finishing this chapter I officiated at a wedding. All week I'd been thinking about the prayer and the petition to "lead us, not into temptation, but deliver us from evil."

Following the exchange of vows and the exchange of rings, I invited the couple to kneel at the kneeler set before the altar. I had them place their hands atop one another's hands and then on my Bible. Then I placed my hands on their hands, and together we prayed. As they knelt, knowing I would soon lead them in the Lord's Prayer, I thought about how important each line of this prayer was to the success of their marriage.

The success of their marriage will depend upon their ability to live into "ours, us, and we" instead of "mine, my, and me." Their love stands its greatest chance of flourishing if together their life is focused on Thine and Thy instead of mine and my, if they seek to do God's will before their own. They will need the bread of life to sustain them and will find joy as they share their physical bread with those in need. And forgiveness? As we noted in the last chapter, no marriage can survive without it. This is why at almost every wedding I read Paul's words from Colossians 3:13 (NIV), "Bear with each other and forgive one another if any of you has a grievance against someone. Forgive as the Lord forgave you."

And though the couple cannot yet see it, and the wedding is scarcely the time to bring it up, they will also each need this prayer, "Lead us, not into temptation, but deliver us from evil." There are many temptations they will face across the course of their married life. As they kneel and we pray this prayer I think, *"Yes, Lord, please lead them, not into temptation, as the devil might seek to lead them, but deliver them from evil."*

One Little Word

Before delving into the subject of temptation, I want to draw your attention to the little Greek word *kai*—it means "and" and it appears at the beginning of both the last line and this line of the prayer. "And forgive us..." "And lead us, not into temptation...." Honestly, I've never paid much attention to the word *And* in this prayer. In fact, I often drop it when reciting the prayer. Before looking at the prayer in the Greek, I assumed it was something that was casually inserted into the prayer. But the word is there intentionally in both of these petitions.

Kai is a conjunction used in Greek to link together ideas, events, places, or people. In the previous line *kai* links together the prayer for "the bread we need" with forgiveness. I wonder if Jesus is connecting our prayer for bread for all of us, with our need for forgiveness as if knowing that we will fail to provide bread for those in need, and that we will at times fail to avail ourselves of the bread of life he offers.

In the line we focus on in this chapter, Jesus connects our request for forgiveness with the petition that God might lead us, might keep us from temptation, and deliver us from evil. Forgive us and lead us. These two petitions go hand in hand.

It is said that Martin Luther went to bed every night praying, "Forgive us our trespasses," and that he woke up every morning praying, "Lead us not into temptation."

The Universality of Temptation

We're all tempted. This is a part of the human condition. Temptation is the lure or the wooing that we feel internally— often fed by others, or by marketing, or by the devil himself — to say, think, or act in ways that are either morally wrong or that are not healthy or helpful for us. Sometimes the temptation is simply to not do anything at all when God is calling us to act. We feel the inward struggle, a wrestling of the thoughts with a desire to do what we know is wrong, or not to do what we know is right. We have a hunger for the thing that tempts us. Consider the seven deadly sins: lust, gluttony, greed, indifference, anger, envy, and pride. Before we commit any acts involving these sins, we are first tempted by the thought of them.

Some temptations are minor. For example, as I was dieting and exercising in an attempt to shed some excess pounds, it was food that most tempted me. Somehow, whenever I am trying to lose weight, the desire for M&M's and ice cream, for French fries and an extra helping of whatever is so very strong. I lost thirty pounds through exercise and eating right. But during the COVID-19 pandemic, I put fifteen of those pounds back on. Trying to keep the weight off is a daily battle. The temptations are always there. This type of temptation may not involve a grave moral wrong, but it is a lure to do something that would make me less healthy.

Other temptations are more clearly a lure to that which is morally wrong—something that damages others as well as ourselves. A former pastor described to me the process by which he was drawn to cheat on his wife. Little by little, the flirtations became fixations; the brief touch became an embrace. These acts eventually led to a full-blown affair, which included no small amount of deception—secrets that my friend kept from his wife and from his congregation. But, once this improper relationship was discovered, the broken trust and deception resulted in both the end of his marriage and the end of his ministry and, for some in his congregation, a loss of their faith.

> Temptation is a universal part of the human condition. The question is not whether we will be tempted, but how we will respond when temptation comes.

We all experience temptation. We're tempted to overconsume, tempted to gossip, tempted to not care, tempted by the desire for more, tempted by the need for affirmation, tempted to want what is not ours, tempted to blow up at one another, tempted to live and think as if the world revolves around us. Temptation is a universal part of the human condition. The question is not whether we will be tempted, but how we will respond when temptation comes.

Genesis 3 contains the archetypal story of temptation, right there as part of the opening story in Scripture. You may recall that the story begins with these words: "Now the serpent was more crafty than any other wild animal that the Lord God had made" (Genesis 3:1 NRSV).

In Genesis 3, Eve encounters a walking, talking snake. The talking snake is the embodiment of temptation. I love how the Scripture notes that he was "more crafty" than any other animal God had made. The Hebrew word is *aram*, and it can mean crafty, but also cunning and even sensible. The serpent was great at rationalizing and making arguments for doing the very thing God had told Adam and Eve not to do. And yet, from a certain point of view, the talking snake's arguments seemed sensible to Eve. The serpent told her, "God knows that when you eat of [the forbidden fruit] your eyes will be opened, and you will be like God, knowing good and evil" (v. 5 NRSV).

The Disney animated adaptation of Rudyard Kipling's *The Jungle Book* gives a nod to this biblical story. There's a scene in which Kaa, the python, hypnotizes the boy, Mowgli, with the intention of devouring him. Hypnosis is an apt metaphor for temptation; it's as if we fall under a spell and become susceptible to suggestion.

I've never seen a talking snake trying to lure me to do what I don't want to do, or what I should not do. But I have often heard the voice of the serpent in my mind seeking to lure me to sin. I hear his whisper rationalizing with me in my secret thoughts, telling me that the very things I know I should not do will be the things that will make me happy. And every time I give in to his whispers, I find the opposite is true.

Whether you perceive the tempter as a literal spiritual being, or merely as the personification of the dark side of your, and others', psyche, there is no denying that we all wrestle with temptation. Within ourselves we've seen that battle and known the arguments back and forth in our minds, in which our conscience and God's Spirit seek to lead us to do what is good and right and just and lovely—and in which another force, power, and voice lure us to do what we should not do. We know how, in the moment, the tempter's arguments sound so alluring that we, like Adam and Eve, at times succumb.

I take comfort in knowing that even Jesus was tempted. Near the beginning of Matthew, Mark, and Luke, Jesus is tempted by the devil. Christians affirm that Jesus was both fully God and fully human. As a man, he was tempted as we are though he alone, among all humans, never succumbed.

Because Jesus resisted the temptations offered by Satan, it's easy for us to miss how intense his wrestling with the devil must have been. Jesus was alone in the wilderness, fasting and praying for forty days and forty nights. He must have been very hungry. Can you hear the tempter, "If you really are God's son, as you thought you heard the voice from heaven say at your baptism, then prove it. You are so hungry, Jesus. Surely your Father doesn't want you to starve. You can break your fast with a morsel of bread. And what's the harm in using your power to turn a rock into a bit of bread?" Notice the "if" (or the CEB has "since")—this is in part about planting seeds of doubt. Jesus responds with a Scripture we read in chapter three: "It is written, 'One does not live by bread alone, but by every word that comes from the mouth of God'" (Matthew 4:4 NRSV).

Then Satan takes him to a high point of the Temple in Jerusalem, and there the devil encourages him to jump, saying, "If you are the Son of God, surely God will deliver you," and then the devil quotes Scripture, Psalm 91:11-12, in which the psalmist promises that God's angels would protect God's people and not allow them to even bruise their foot upon the stones. Was this a temptation to an amazing stunt that would prove to Jesus and others that he really was the Son of God? Was it a way out of the path of suffering that lay ahead? By doing this, Jesus would either be delivered by God or die. Either way he would avoid the road that ended in a cross. Once more Jesus quotes Scripture in response to the temptation, "Don't test the Lord your God."

Then the devil offers him earthly power—the kingdoms of this world if he'll only turn aside from following God and bow before the devil. It is interesting that Jesus's prayer speaks of the kingdom belonging to his Father. Here the devil seeks to lead Jesus to focus on my and mine, not Thy and Thine. And at what cost? Worshiping Satan over God? Once more Jesus refuses to succumb, again quoting Scripture in response to the temptation, "You shall worship the Lord your God and serve only him" (Matthew 4:10).

By the way, it's interesting to me that in the second of the temptations, the devil quotes Scripture to Jesus when attempting to lure him to turn from God's path. Even the devil can quote Scripture. And just because someone quotes Scripture does not mean they are leading you in the right path.

Have you ever thought about how the temptations actually occurred? Do you imagine the devil showed up wearing red spandex tights, pitchfork in hand? I don't think that would have been tempting for Jesus. No, I suspect that he tempted Jesus the way he tempts us—as the voice in our head, whispering, arguing, rationalizing, seeking to lure us to do what we know we should not do.

As Kaa seeks to devour Mowgli, the devil is described in Scripture as one seeking to devour God's people. This is why 1 Peter 5:8-9 notes, "Like a roaring lion your adversary the devil prowls around looking for someone to devour. Resist him, steadfast in your faith."

So, like Jesus, we know temptation. And we know that many of the worst decisions in our lives, those that caused pain to ourselves or others, came when we listened to the voice of the tempter, and succumbed to the alluring rationalizations of the adversary.

Paul likens this wrestling match for our hearts and minds, this spiritual warfare, to actual combat. In Ephesians 6:10-11 he invokes the language of battle and armament, telling his readers: "Finally, be strengthened by the Lord and his powerful strength.

Put on God's armor so that you can make a stand against the tricks of the devil." He goes on to list the armor we use in this kind of spiritual battle: the belt of truth, justice as a breastplate, shoes that represent the sharing of the gospel, a shield that is faith, a helmet of salvation, and the sword of the Spirit. Paul understands that temptation is going to be a struggle. He wants us to be well-equipped for what is inevitably coming.

An Odd Petition

Recognizing the battles we all face with temptation, we return to Jesus's prayer. He tells us to pray, "Lead us, not into temptation, but deliver us from evil." One of the members of the congregation I serve wrote a note to ask me, "I've never understood why we need to pray for God to not lead us into temptation. Why would God lead us into temptation to begin with? And if there was some good reason for him to lead us into temptation, why would we pray that he would not do the thing he knew was best for us?"

These are great questions. You may have pondered them yourself. They were questions that early followers of Jesus also apparently asked. In his letter, James addresses them like this: "No one who is tested should say, 'God is tempting me!' This is because God is not tempted by any form of evil, nor does he tempt anyone" (James 1:13). So God does not tempt us to do what is wrong. God wants to encourage us to do what is right. David had it right when he wrote of God in Psalm 23, "He leadeth me in the paths of righteousness for his name's sake" (v. 3b KJV).

104

So, if God leads us to do what is right, and does not lead us to do what is wrong, then what sense does it make to pray, "Lead us not into temptation"? One commentator I read years ago, I've long since forgotten who, noted that the problem isn't with the prayer, but how we pray it. Specifically, he noted, there is a missing comma in the line.

We typically pray the prayer like this: "Lead us not into temptation." Heard this way, we naturally interpret the petition to mean something like: "Please, God, don't lead us into places where we'll be tempted." And it raises the question my parishioner was asking: Why would a loving God want to do that?

Now hear it with a comma (you might even try reading it aloud): "Lead us, [pause] not into temptation, but deliver us from evil." It changes how we understand the petition. Now the emphasis is on "lead us," as it should be. It is even more helpful if we understand that Jesus is asking us to pray to our Father to lead us, while it is the tempter, either within or without, who leads us into temptation. So think of the prayer this way: "Lead us, not into temptation as the tempter, or we ourselves, might lead, but deliver us from evil (or, as some translations have it, the evil one). The focus of this petition is that God lead us.

I wonder if you ever lead yourself into temptation. I had a parishioner who described his battle with pornography. He didn't want to look at it and always felt crummy afterward. He didn't believe this was God's will for him. But he would dabble at internet searches that were likely to turn up websites that were pornographic and then be unable to resist looking at them. I remember another parishioner who was a recovering alcoholic who had fallen off the wagon a few times. She told me she would go to the bar to order soda, just to prove she could. But many times she ended up sitting there until she could resist it no more, and then finally ordered a drink. It wasn't God leading these two on their internet search or the trip to the bar. They were leading themselves, or the tempter was leading them.

Lead us. I love the prayer implied by the twenty-third psalm: "Lead us in the paths of righteousness. Lead us beside the still waters." Or the words of Thomas Dorsey's well-loved hymn: "Precious Lord, take my hand, lead me on, let me stand."[2] In the Lord's Prayer we are asking God to lead us as opposed to our leading ourselves. Twenty-five years ago, I began trying to retrain our congregation to insert the comma to make this clear "And lead us"—pause—"not into temptation"—pause—"but deliver us from evil." It took months before they got used to it, but now it sounds strange to say it any other way.

In the Lord's Prayer we are asking God to lead us as opposed to our leading ourselves.

I was grateful when Pope Francis wrote his own book on the Lord's Prayer several years ago and shared that he'd concluded Christians had been praying the prayer wrong. He noted that God doesn't lead us into temptation, and hence this line of the prayer is focused on inviting God to lead us. Left to our own devices, we'll lead ourselves into temptation. I loved this, as the Pope was catching up with what we'd been teaching the folks at Resurrection for years. We were glad to see the Catholics joining us Methodists in seeing it this way!

I mentioned earlier my love of M&M's. Sometime ago I was at a CVS Pharmacy, and I noted they had dark chocolate peanut M&M's on sale for a great price. At the time, I had given up M&M's as part of my effort to lose weight. But the special offer on "sharing sized" bags, buy one, get one free, was irresistibly tempting. It was such a great deal. So I thought, well, I just can't pass up this opportunity. I bought all ten of the 8.3 ounce bags they had on the shelf! Eighty-three ounces, FIVE POUNDS of dark chocolate peanut M&M's!

In my office at church, I have an M&M's jar one of our parishioners gave me. "M&M's" is actually printed on the side. The jar had sat empty for months while I resisted the temptation. But now that I had bags of M&M's, the jar seemed to need filling. I had kept the empty jar ten feet away on a bookshelf. But now that I had filled the jar, I decided that it might look better on my desk. And so it migrated over from the shelf. Then I decided, as I was working on a sermon, that I could indulge myself by eating just four M&M's. But four soon became eight, and eight became sixteen. I told myself that dark chocolate is good for you. Peanuts are good for you, too. And before long, I was all the way down at the bottom of the slippery M&M's slope. Bite by bite, I wound up consuming the entire jar—eight hundred calories of dark chocolate peanut M&M's in one sitting, which definitely was *not* good for me and left me with a stomachache.

I've been doing better when it comes to M&M's, but I had to laugh as I was preparing the final revisions to this chapter, for, as I sat down to work, I had grabbed the Family Size bag (19.2 ounces) of dark chocolate peanut M&M's I had in the pantry, not recalling that I'd included my temptation with M&M's in this chapter I was preparing to review. (Thanks to re-reading this chapter, I ate only one serving, thirteen pieces, before zipping up the bag and putting it away.)

God did not lead me into this temptation. I led myself there. But a jar of dark chocolate M&M's is one thing. In the grand scheme of things, that is one relatively minor temptation. Is it possible the more serious temptations are reflected earlier in this prayer? Is it the decision over whether we'll go about our lives focused on my and mine instead of Thy and Thine? Is it whether we'll seek God's will and kingdom or our own? Is it being satisfied with mere bread and missing out on the *epiousian* bread that satisfies our hearts? Or choosing to harbor bitterness and resentment rather than releasing our grievances?

The underlying presupposition in this prayer, and in the Christian life, is that God will lead us if we ask. In essence this is what it means to be a Christian. To be a Christian is to be a follower of Christ. Jesus gave this invitation, "Come and follow me." He said, "If any would be my disciples, they must take up their cross and follow me" (see Luke 9:23). To call Jesus Lord is to call him our sovereign, our king, our ruler, our leader. To be a disciple is to be a follower. So, the Christian life is lived seeking to follow him.

I love that old gospel hymn with the chorus, "Where he leads me I will follow, where he leads me I will follow, where he leads me I will follow. I'll go with him, with him all the way."[3] Every time I pray this prayer, I'm asking God to lead me. I'm inviting him to turn me from the temptation I'm so easily drawn to.

How does God lead us? By the Holy Spirit—that nudge we feel and hear in our hearts. And God leads us by means of the Scriptures, as we saw modeled by Jesus in his response to the tempter. God leads us as we pray, meditate, and listen. God leads us as we worship, when we join others in small groups, and in a host of other ways. The key is learning to listen. Lead us, not into temptation.

"Save Us from the Evil One"

Temptation is a powerful pull to do what harms us. It discredits our witness and integrity, and it can influence us to do harm to others. It is the lure to do what will separate us from God and what will keep us from doing God's will.

As noted earlier, the Bible personifies temptation, the lure of darkness and evil, by speaking of the devil, also known as Satan (or *the* Satan), the adversary, the accuser, the serpent, the tempter, and the enemy. In his book, *The Screwtape Letters*, C. S. Lewis captures well the "wiles of the devil" as Paul describes them in Ephesians 6. Lewis also suggests that the devil's favorite strategy for tripping Christians up is to try to convince people he does not exist.

I'm confident that I'm quite capable of leading myself into temptation; I don't need the devil's help. But I find it helpful to think of the devil as the embodiment of temptation, evil, and the lure of darkness; as the dark side or the force of darkness in my life and in the world. It is important to recognize that in the Scriptures, he is no match for God. And no match for the Spirit's leading in our lives, providing we're inviting God to lead us. But he's great at tripping us up if we're not inviting God to lead.

The devil cannot make us do anything, but he does have the power of suggestion and he seems to know each of our weaknesses. C. H. Spurgeon, an eminent nineteenth-century British pastor, described Satan's work of tempting by likening him to a fisherman who "watches his fish, adapts his bait to his prey, and knows in what seasons the fish are most likely to bite."[4]

Jesus calls us to not only pray, "Lead us, not into temptation," but also, "deliver us from evil." The Greek word for "deliver" is *rhyomai*; our English word *rush* is derived from this word. So this petition in the prayer is a call for God to rush to us, to rescue us, or deliver us, or snatch us out of the hands of evil.

Matthew has the little word "the" (*tou* in Greek) just before evil. Deliver us from "the evil" it literally reads in Greek. This leads many modern translators to translate this line as, "Deliver us from the evil one"—from the tempter, from the evil one that would destroy us. But *tou ponerou,* as "the evil" is in the Greek, can simply be rendered as the bad, the hurtful, or that which is morally or ethically wrong.

In both the Old and New Testaments, we find the imagery of God shepherding his people, and part of that shepherding is leading the animals to safety. Part of shepherding includes protecting animals from their predators. In this prayer we're inviting God, our shepherd, to both lead us and protect us from harm.

In this prayer we're inviting God, our shepherd, to both lead us and protect us from harm.

I think of a video that went viral recently of a man in Florida whose dog strayed close to a pond in his back yard. Ponds can be a dangerous spot in a place like Florida. Suddenly, with no warning, a juvenile alligator emerged from the pond, seized the startled dog, and carried it under the water. Almost as quickly, the dog's owner jumped into the water and grabbed the gator. He pried open the reptile's jaws so that his dog, a King Charles Cavalier spaniel who had not yet been seriously injured, was able to escape safely to shore. Then the man released the alligator, got out of the pond, picked up the fortunate dog, and walked away. Evil always lurks near us, but God is always by our side. "Rush to us, Lord, and rescue us before we are devoured by the evil that is never far away."

The story reminds me once again of 1 Peter 5:8-9: "Be clear-headed. Keep alert. Your accuser, the devil, is on the prowl like a roaring lion, seeking someone to devour. Resist him, standing firm in the faith." Peter was addressing Christians who were suffering, and the devil was himself personified as the source of their suffering. We can pray that God will deliver us from evil, and the evil one, from hardship and adversity.

But once again we play a part in fulfilling our prayers: *ora et labora*, pray and work. Inviting God to lead you, and not following the voice of the tempter, is the key strategy to being delivered from evil. We have two voices vying for our heart, the voice of the Good Shepherd and the voice of the tempter. The question is always, which voice will we listen to?

James describes temptation using the metaphor of conception, gestation, and birth: "Everyone is tempted by their own cravings; they are lured away and enticed by them. Once those cravings conceive, they give birth to sin; and when sin grows up, it gives birth to death" (James 1:14-15).

It would take more than one book to recount the stories of people I have known and ministered with whose lives were wrecked by listening to the wrong voice.

I think of a woman who was caught stealing from her company. She was not a bad person. But the voice had rationalized the act, telling her she was underpaid, and she deserved what she was taking. "No one will miss it." She listened to the wrong voice, was caught by the security cameras, lost the job she loved, and experienced a great deal of pain because she listened to the voice of the tempter.

I think of the man who was a serial adulterer. He knew it was wrong, that it would devastate his wife if she found out, that he would lose the respect and love of his children, and that it might lead to contracting a sexually transmitted disease affecting not only his own health but that of his wife as well. In the end he did lose his wife and kids when they discovered the alternate life he was leading. The result was great pain: *tou ponerou*—the evil, the painful, the bad, the wicked, the toilsome, the evil one. Lead us, not into temptation, but *deliver us from evil.*

Lead *Us*, Not into Temptation, but Deliver *Us* from Evil

Up to this point we've been thinking of temptation and evil in personal terms. While we've not said it, our focus has been on the idea of our praying, "Lead *me*, not into temptation, but deliver *me* from evil." But once more we must remember that Jesus taught us to pray, "ours, us, and we," not "mine, my, and me." In what ways do communities or whole societies find themselves tempted or seduced by evil or the evil one?

We can look back in history and see times when tribes, nations, and masses of people were seduced by evil and in turn became instruments of evil, injustice, cruelty, or inhumanity. This has been true as long as there have been humans on the earth. Neanderthals became extinct between 37,000 and 40,000 years ago. One hypothesis suggests that their extinction was in part a result of warfare with and slaughter by modern humans, whose brains and physiology gave them an advantage over the Neanderthals. History is littered with the story of war and genocide.

The Old Testament bears witness to this violence nations and peoples committed against one another. The slaughter of entire cities, tribes, and people is described in Joshua. In 2 Samuel 11:1 we read, rather matter-of-factly, "In the spring, when kings go off to war, David sent Joab, along with his servants and all the Israelites, and they destroyed the Ammonites, attacking the city of Rabbah." Springtime came, and kings led their troops on a killing spree in order to subject the people, and take the property, of neighboring kingdoms. The nations of the ancient Near East believed they went into battle with the encouragement and blessings of their gods.

Israel's story as described in the Hebrew Bible is marked by aggression and oppression at the hands of her neighbors, and sometimes toward her neighbors. Then there were the major empires whose armies marched against God's people, demanding tribute payment from and ruling over them. Israel's conquerors included the Egyptians, Assyrians, Babylonians, Persians, Greeks, and Romans—all took their turn at subjugating and controlling the people of Israel and Judah.

Despite following a Lord who commanded his disciples to love their enemies, Christians succumbed to the use of violence against their enemies. Crusades and countless other wars and acts of violence have been waged by followers of the Prince of Peace.

Among the temptations Christian societies succumbed to was the lure of anti-Semitism. I was in Germany on the five hundredth anniversary of Martin Luther's posting of the Ninety-Five Theses to the door of the Wittenberg Castle Church, what is considered the beginning of the Protestant Reformation. While there visiting medieval towns, I witnessed more than nine centuries of anti-Semitism. Look up the word *Judensau* online and look carefully at the image. For hundreds of years starting in the 1200s, if not earlier, the image of Jews eating the excrement of a sow and sucking on its teats was considered amusing and somehow appropriate as art in Christian churches. Visit the Church of St. Mary in Wittenberg, the city church where Luther preached, and you'll find a Judensau bas relief on the side of the church building, placed there in 1305.

Luther at first condemned the cruel treatment of Jews by Christians, writing and speaking forcefully against it (see his 1523 *That Jesus Christ Was Born a Jew*), but twenty years later, in 1543, he wrote a tragic book called *On the Jews and Their Lies*, in which he described the Jewish people in terms I won't repeat here, calling for synagogues and Jewish schools to be burned and the wealth of Jews to be confiscated, returned to them only if they converted.

Four hundred years later, the book was held up as an example by the Nazis claiming Luther as a champion of their views. As I write these words, I'm looking at the photos I took in the crematorium of the Buchenwald Concentration Camp. Over 50,000 people are believed to have died in this camp. Cruel and inhumane experiments were carried out there. It was, like so many other Nazi camps, illustrative of the evil humans are capable of. If only Christians had taken seriously the words Luther claimed to pray each morning, "Lead us, not into temptation, but deliver us from evil."

I wondered, as I stood on these grounds, how many of the guards, the administrators, the leadership of the Nazi party would have called themselves Christians? A survey in 1939, six years after the Nazis came to power, found that 94 percent of Germans claimed to be Christians and another 3.5 percent claimed to believe in God. There are examples of courageous Christians who opposed the Reich (I'll mention one in the concluding chapter), including those who worked to hide and save Jews from the camps. But so many more were silent, or somehow justified the slaughter of six million Jews and the many others who died at the hands of the Nazis. *Lead us, not into temptation, but deliver us from evil!*

I think also of the Rwandan genocide of 1994, when at least a half a million Tutsis and moderate Hutus were killed by their neighbors over one hundred days that spring. Ninety-two percent of the population were Christians. Christians had come to believe the lies of their leaders, that Tutsis were somehow less than human. Stories abound of people killing their fellow church members, neighbors, and co-workers with machetes, weapons that had been purchased en masse and hidden just for this purpose. How could this happen among Christian people? *Lead us, not into temptation, but deliver us from evil!*

But this is not simply a problem with "those people" "over there." Most of you reading this book live in the U.S. Throughout our nation's history our population has been majority Christian. We can look back and see things from a perspective that our forebearers could not. The history of European Americans and their treatment of Native Americans is a history of broken treaties and trails of tears. Most of those Euro-Americans claimed to be followers of Jesus.

Consider capturing or purchasing Africans and forcing them on slave ships where they would be sold to eager buyers in

America, laborers owned by their masters and, at times, beaten into submission. How many in the slave trade, those selling and the customers purchasing these slaves, would have claimed a Christian faith? Jim Crow, "Separate but Equal," the KKK, and ongoing racism and bigotry bear witness to the insidious power of the evil one and the darkness within. *Lead us, Lord, not into temptation as we're so prone to go, and deliver us from evil!*

Where are the places where you see Christians embracing darkness instead of light today? accepting lies as if they are true? embracing ideologies and political ideas that are the opposite of Christ while rationalizing that these are consistent with their faith? Christians tend to answer these questions differently depending upon where they live in our country, their education and socioeconomic status, their race, and their politics.

The polarization of America leaves us ripe for what Paul calls the "devil's tricks."

The polarization of America leaves us ripe for what Paul calls the "devil's tricks." I'd suggest "the devil" has us precisely where he wants us. We tune in to news sources that confirm our biases. We find it easy to believe the worst about the political other. We dismiss news and information that is counter to our biases as "fake news." Conspiracy theories abound.

In this prayer Jesus beckons us to pray both for ourselves, "Lead us, not into temptation, but deliver us from evil," and also for our society, our nation, and our world. Lead *us*, not into temptation, but deliver *us* from evil.

Jesus knew the internal struggle with temptation. He understood the lure of the evil one who sought to derail him as he began his ministry. He knew that his followers would struggle personally with temptation and evil. And he knew how societies would struggle with the enticement to evil.

We need this prayer, personally, as we strive to listen and follow the voice of the Spirit and not the whisper of the serpent. But *we* also need it as the church, God's people, that we will not be deceived, but instead courageously follow Christ. In this time in which we live, the world needs us to not only pray, but to live this prayer...

> *Our Father, who art in heaven, hallowed be thy name.*
> *Thy kingdom come, thy will be done on earth as it is in heaven.*
> *Give us this day our daily bread.*
> *And forgive us our trespasses, as we forgive those who trespass against us.*
> *And* lead us, *not into temptation, but* deliver us from evil.
> *For thine is the kingdom, and the power, and the glory, forever.*
> *Amen.*

6

For Thine Is the Kingdom, Power, and Glory

6

FOR THINE IS THE KINGDOM, POWER, AND GLORY

"After this manner therefore pray ye: Our Father which art in heaven, Hallowed be thy name.

Thy kingdom come, Thy will be done in earth, as it is in heaven.

Give us this day our daily bread.

And forgive us our debts, as we forgive our debtors.

And lead us not into temptation, but deliver us from evil: For thine is the kingdom, and the power, and the glory, for ever. Amen."

(Matthew 6:9b-13 KJV)

This book began as a sermon series, the third sermon series on the Lord's Prayer that I have preached in thirty years. After writing this book, I intend to preach on the prayer far more often. I am convinced that this prayer summarizes so much that was essential to Jesus, and praying it daily has the power to change our lives.

After preaching the most recent series of sermons, I received numerous emails from members of my congregation, describing what the Lord's Prayer meant to them.

One man wrote:

> Two years ago, I had an excellent opportunity to focus on the only thing I could remember from the Bible—the Lord's Prayer—as I was locked up over Labor Day weekend in solitary—the "drunk tank." So I repeated and repeated the Lord's Prayer and felt him join me there in that orange cell with a hole in the floor. His presence and comfort kept me warm and gave me the strength to stop drinking after a five-year bender. Sober two years twelve days. I pray every day that the Lord's work be done on earth and that he uses me to do his work with what skills and talents I have.

A woman wrote:

> My mother's cancer returned last summer, and it overcame her fairly quickly. I was blessed enough to be able to be there with my family those last few days. In her final moments, I sat at her bedside with my Dad and sister. I knew it was time to pray, so I asked my Dad to lead us in the Lord's Prayer. My mother literally took one last breath after the prayer and then she passed.

The woman went on to share that, in the months prior to her mother's death, the words of the prayer were little more than a bunch of phrases she had memorized when she was ten. But in the months after that, she said, everything changed. She had been one of the nominally religious persons who start attending the church I pastor, returning to faith. At the age of forty-nine, one year after her mother died, she was baptized. In her note she wrote that, she now prayed "the Lord's Prayer with clarity and conviction." She wrote that her life had been transformed during the course of a year and that she was now able to say the Lord's Prayer and mean it.

We've seen how this prayer is meant to become such a part of us that it shapes and defines our lives.

We have a service once a month at Church of the Resurrection for persons suffering from Alzheimer's and dementia. Many of those in attendance do not remember their own names. But when we get to the time in the service when we pray the Lord's Prayer, many of them join in. While they've lost most of their memories, these words, which they recited so many times across the course of their lives, have been inscribed upon their hearts and minds in such a way that even Alzheimer's or dementia has not been able to erase them.

The prayer crosses all boundaries erected by human beings.

Across the trenches on the battle fields of Europe during World War I—at times British soldiers would be close enough that, if the evening was quiet and the wind was right, they could hear their enemies. There were times soldiers reported hearing their German counterparts, saying the Lord's Prayer in unison. They didn't understand the language. But they recognized the familiar rhythm of the words, "*Vater unsere im Himmel, geheiligt werde dein Name.*" And so, in English, they joined their enemies in reciting the Lord's Prayer.

My hope was that by focusing on the Lord's Prayer in this book, and inviting you to pray it daily, it might come to be inscribed on *your* heart, that it might shape your life, and that it would be one of the anchors of your soul as you grow older.

In this final chapter we will look at the closing line of the Lord's Prayer: "For thine is the kingdom, and the power, and the glory, forever." As we learned in the introduction, scholars call a line such as this a "doxology." It likely was not originally a part of the prayer that Jesus taught, though by the end of the first century Christians were reciting this or something very close to it as a shout of praise in response to the prayer (while not originally in Matthew or Luke's account of the prayer, it was already a part of the prayer when the *Didache* was written, possibly before the end of the first century). Short words of praise are common throughout the Bible, and this doxology was inspired by King David's words recorded in 1 Chronicles 29:11 (KJV):

> Thine, O LORD, is the greatness, and the power, and
> the glory, and the victory, and the majesty: for all
> that is in the heaven and in the earth is thine; thine
> is the kingdom, O LORD, and thou art exalted as
> head above all.

While many modern translations now include this only in a footnote, I did not want to end our study of the Lord's Prayer without a look at the meaning of this doxological conclusion to it.

For Thine...

The doxology begins with the word *for*. This little preposition is saying, in essence, the reason we can pray for all of these things in the Lord's Prayer is *for* or *because* the kingdom, power, and glory already belong to God. God is our Father in heaven, the author of creation. All things belong to God, who made them. When we pray the words of this doxology, we not only acknowledge God's power; we are also making a statement of faith: "Because yours is the kingdom, the power, and glory, O God, I know that you are with me and hear my prayer. I know that you are able to provide for our daily needs. I know that you can rescue us from evil. I know that you forgive the debts that imprison us, freeing us to spread that forgiveness to others."

We learned in an earlier chapter that, when we say *Thine* in the Lord's Prayer, it is a declaration, a decision of the will that runs in direct contrast to the natural tendency of our heart to say *mine*. Once more, when we come to the doxology to the Lord's Prayer, we are choosing Thy and Thine instead of my and mine.

Saying this prayer daily, with its doxology, is a way of shaping and training our hearts, as we pray, "Thine, not mine, O God, is the kingdom. Thine, not mine, is the power. Thine, not mine is the glory. I'm yielding my little kingdom, whatever power I have, and whatever glory I might have sought, to you." Once more the prayer leads us to one of the central questions of our faith: Will our life be focused on mine or Thine?

When our doxology—our daily prayer—is mine, we live small and narcissistic lives. But when we lose our lives for God's sake, when we lay down our crowns, when we stop craving power, and when we give God the glory instead of seeking it for ourselves, we live large, magnanimous lives.

> **When we lose our lives for God's sake, when we lay down our crowns, when we stop craving power, and when we give God the glory instead of seeking it for ourselves, we live large, magnanimous lives.**

Jesus was trying to teach us this lesson when, at the Last Supper, he told his disciples that the truly great among them would see themselves as servants. He made the point, despite Peter's protestations, when he washed his disciples' feet that night. And he made the point again when he prayed in the garden a short time later, "Not my will, but yours be done." Finally, he demonstrated what this looked like as he hung on the cross, giving his life for the debts of the world.

Is the Kingdom

"For thine is the kingdom." In considering this statement, Bishop William Willimon and Duke University ethics professor Stanley Hauerwas wrote, "Here come politics again, one more time as we end our attempt to pray as Jesus taught us." They note that the Lord's Prayer, particularly this line, is a "pledge of allegiance to a king and his kingdom that throws all our allegiances into crisis."[1] Have you ever thought of the Lord's Prayer, and this last line, in this way? It is a pledge of our allegiance to God's kingdom, power, and glory. This pledge and this allegiance to God's kingdom, power, and glory are meant to come before all other allegiances in our lives.

Chuck Colson, the special counsel to President Richard Nixon, served seven months in prison for his role in obstructing justice related to the Watergate scandal. Shortly before his prison sentence began, he became a follower of Jesus Christ. After his release, he became a thoughtful Christian leader. In his 1987 book, *Kingdoms in Conflict,* he noted that, throughout history, the church with its pledge to the kingdom of God has often come in conflict with the kingdoms of this earth.

I mentioned Nazi Germany in the last chapter. While many Christians participated in the Nazi regime, or were simply silent in the face of its activity, Colson noted that there were faithful Christians who resisted, precisely because of their allegiance to God's kingdom. Colson noted, "Nazi files clearly record that the church struggle was a constant thorn in the flesh to Hitler and his aides during their early years in power.... It was a credit to the church's reliance on an ultimate authority and vision quite apart from the political order" that led Christians "to resist Hitler's blasphemous claims, even when his political popularity was soaring." The church, Colson noted, was "the only institution in Germany that offered any enduring or meaningful resistance."[2]

In 1987, a man named Pierre Sauvage made a film about his birthplace, an isolated French village called Le Chambon-sur-Lignon. Sauvage, his parents, and at least five thousand Jews survived because their Christian neighbors organized to protect them from discovery by the Nazis and deportation to concentration camps that would inevitably follow. Sauvage made his film, *Weapons of the Spirit*, in an attempt to understand why an entire community would have put itself at mortal risk to save others.

Sauvage learned of a sermon preached by the local pastor, whose words helped galvanize the villagers: "The duty of the Christians is to resist the violence that will be brought to bear on their consciences through the weapons of the spirit. We shall resist when our adversaries shall demand of us obedience contrary to the orders of the Gospel. We shall do so without fear, but also without pride and without hatred."

And that is what this community of mostly poor farmers did. They took Jewish refugees into their homes. They lied to the authorities. They set up an underground railroad to smuggle Jews across the border into neutral Switzerland.

Engaging in what Sauvage labeled a "conspiracy of goodness," the villagers offered such a powerful witness through their actions that, as word spread through quiet, back channels, Jews from other areas of France made their way to Le Chambon for protection; eventually, there were as many Jews in the area as French Christians. Local officials of the Vichy government, which cooperated elsewhere with the German occupiers in rounding up Jews, joined in the "conspiracy." After discovering the rescue effort, even some of the German soldiers and officers stationed in the area chose to help keep the secret rather than reporting to their superiors what was happening in Le Chambon. In this way all of these people faced allegiances in crisis—and chose God's kingdom over earthly powers. As Sauvage came to believe, when people concertedly engage in goodness, it becomes contagious, spreading in unforeseen, unimaginable ways, even into the hearts of enemies who are converted into co-conspirators.[3]

Despite such efforts, many church people, and many of their pastors and leaders, capitulated to Hitler. They wished not to rock the boat or, worse, actually embraced Nazi rhetoric. In the end, Colson wrote, "[As many in the churches supported] Hitler's schemes, the church failed to hold the state to account."[4] Ninety percent of the people in Nazi Germany were Christians who prayed the Lord's Prayer, yet they failed to understand or live what they were praying.

One cannot help but wonder, had the German population understood this prayer, had they said no to the Holocaust, had they refused to support the Nazi aggression against their European neighbors, what would have happened? How might history have been different? It is estimated that one out of every thirty-three people on the planet died directly or indirectly as a result of the Holocaust and the Second World War. How many millions would have lived had more people taken seriously their pledge of allegiance to God and God's kingdom? How many could have been saved from weapons of war by the deployment of the weapons of the Spirit?

Today, our praying this prayer, pledging our allegiance to God and God's kingdom, means that we must ask probing questions of our nation and of our leaders: "Is this law, this piece of legislation, this executive order, this policy, consistent with the values we have pledged ourselves to in the Lord's Prayer?" Is my support of this policy, this law, this position, consistent with my pledge recognizing that the kingdom, power, and glory belong to God and God alone?

Karl Barth, one of the great twentieth-century theologians, was right when he famously said, "To clasp the hands in prayer is the beginning of an uprising against the disorder of the world." Our prayer is meant to impact our politics and policies. It is meant to resolve the conflict of our allegiances.

The Power

The Greek word we translate as *power* is *dynamis*, from which we have our word *dynamite*. *Dynamis* and its Hebrew equivalent appear hundreds of times in the Bible. What do we mean by power? It is the influence, authority, strength, force, or capacity to accomplish something or get something done. In attributing *dynamis* to God we are recognizing both that God literally is the power by which all things exist and also that God is the rightful authority or ruler of all.

Each of us also has power. God shares his power with us. Jesus promised the disciples that when the Holy Spirit came upon them, they would have power. They, and we, would have power to be his witnesses. We have power to influence, power to act, power to do his work. We can use this Spirit's power to impact others' lives and the world around us.

We also have another kind of power: the power of our position in the workplace, our economic means, our influence with others, our relationships, our physical strength. Even our vote is a form of power.

We can use this second kind of power wisely and well, or we can misuse and abuse our power. We can use our power for good or evil ends; for selfless or selfish ends. Once more the question is, mine or Thine?

Power is seductive. It is alluring. It tempts us. Earthly power, as we read in the previous chapter, is one of the temptations that Satan dangled before Jesus in the wilderness. The Romans used to say that "Money is like salt water: The more you drink, the thirstier you get." Chuck Colson restated this as, "Power is like saltwater; the more you drink, the thirstier you get."[5] For many people, a little power leads them on a "power trip."

You probably know Lord Acton's famous dictum, "Power tends to corrupt, and absolute power corrupts absolutely." But do you know the context of that quote? It was a letter to a bishop of the Church of England. Acton was writing about the popes who encouraged and supported the Inquisition to arrest, torture, and kill people they labeled as heretics (especially Jews). And then he moved from there to discuss the ways that powerful people in his own country, including kings and queens, had abused their secular power to harm others.[6]

But it's not just the medieval popes and national rulers who misused power and were corrupted by it. The #MeToo movement brought into the open the misuse and abuse of power, typically by men against their subordinates, often women, to gratify their own desires. It's what we see in families where there is physical or emotional abuse by a parent. It is the misuse of power by law enforcement, something the world saw as a police officer knelt on the neck of George Floyd until he died. It is the misuses of power by clergy who harm the people entrusted to their care. What Lord Acton warned against is seen anywhere in the world that the powerful exploit their power for their own ends and oppress those they are meant to protect.

When we pray *Thine*, not mine, we commit to use our power and influence for God's good purposes.

But power can also be used for good. When we pray *Thine*, not mine, we commit to use our power and influence for God's good purposes. As we yield it to God, we begin to hear God calling us to use our power to, in the words of the popular version of the Second General Rule of the early Methodist movement, "do all the good that you can, to everyone that you can, everywhere that you can, as often as you can."

In the summer of 2020, at the height of the COVID-19 pandemic, our congregation was holding Vacation Bible Camp online. We'd never done this before, but we managed to hold a meaningful week of programming to help our children grow in their faith. Each year our Vacation Bible Camp has a mission focus, and the kids give an offering to the service project. That year we were partnering with Methodist churches in Malawi. I mentioned earlier in this book our visit with tribal elders in villages in Malawi, who had been praying for safe drinking water for their children. Our congregation has been funding the drilling of wells ever since.

Our mission focus in Vacation Bible Camp was to raise money for several more wells for villages that still did not have access to clean water. The pastors and mission workers in Malawi sent phone video footage of their kids teaching our children their favorite songs and games. Our kids shared videos back in return. Our children were able to see the open pits and muddy water these children had to use to bathe, cook, and drink. They went about raising funds to provide for wells, raising funds for three "bore holes."

Among the activities the children participated in to understand life in Malawi was to carry five-gallon buckets partially filled with water. In this way, they could experience a small part of the daily life of children in Malawi. Six-year-old Hudson carried one of these buckets down his street. He did this despite battling a brain tumor that made it even more difficult to carry the bucket, a tumor that would claim his life several months later. When it came time to give his offering, he gave all the money he had to help build a well for the kids in Malawi. It was deeply moving to hear what he had done.

After Vacation Bible Camp, we shared with our congregation that our children had given enough, including Hudson, to provide clean drinking water for three villages in Malawi. Inspired by the children's generosity, their parents and the rest of our adults began giving and soon there were dozens of additional villages in Malawi receiving new wells. It was beautiful, and a glimpse of what it means to pray, Thine is the power. But it was also a powerful picture of so many other things we pray in this prayer. God's name was hallowed. God's kingdom came to each of these villages, and in the hearts of those who gave for the wells. God's will was done. Villages receive their daily bread in the form of clean water. Our members received the daily bread of meaning and joy by helping with these projects. It was a remarkable thing to witness.

The Glory

Finally, in the doxology of the Lord's Prayer there is the glory—the *doxa* (in Greek) or *kavod* (in Hebrew)—of God. The word appears more than 480 times in Hebrew and Greek in the Bible. It means "weight," "reputation," "splendor," "impressiveness," "majesty."

In some ways this also takes us back to the opening petition of the prayer when we pray, "hallowed be thy name." You'll remember that this petition is, in essence, asking God to use us to hallow his name. We're meant to bring honor and glory to God in the eyes of others by how we live.

As we pray, "Thine is the glory," once more we are intentionally countering the natural tendency in our lives to seek glory for ourselves. As we've learned there is a tendency within each of us to want to hallow our own names. We crave the glory. We want the credit for the good things we do. We want people to be impressed by us. We want people to think highly of us. We can brag (or, sometimes, "humble-brag"), show off, and work hard to impress others. We crave affirmation and applause, ribbons and prizes, recognition and praise. That's not true of everyone, of course. Some people are very shy and want to remain in the background. They're often the people who make anonymous gifts and donations because it's not about them. But many are driven by the need for recognition, praise, and glory.

When I was in seminary and a church youth director, I noticed that one of the other youth pastors in Dallas seemed to be copying all of my ideas. His youth newsletter borrowed our graphics. His message to his kids in the newsletter mirrored my own. His talks began to cover the same themes that I had just recently covered. His programming ideas looked almost identical to ones we had implemented for our youth group. By way of complaint, I mentioned this to my senior pastor. Perhaps I imagined that he would go speak to his counterpart at the other church, who would tell the copycat youth director to cease and desist. Instead, he taught me something really important. He said, "Adam, you'll be so much happier in life, and you'll see so much more good happen, if you decide you don't care who gets the credit."

I cringed as he told me that, embarrassed as he pointed out my pride. But he was right. And from that time on I began to celebrate if someone borrowed an idea from me or the church. When we started Church of the Resurrection we made it part of our mission to give away our best ideas. For over twenty years, Church of the Resurrection has hosted a "Leadership Institute" where we give away whatever we've developed for ministry, inviting people to use anything we share that is helpful to them. At each of these gatherings, our aim is to do what my mentor, Bob Robertson, taught me that day: to share our best ideas and not care who gets the credit. Thine is the glory.

Again and again, the Bible notes that the glory belongs to God. We either obscure God's glory, or we reflect it and magnify it. I like to go for walks late at night, and when there is a full moon I don't need a flashlight. The moon reflects the light of the sun.

During a lunar eclipse, on the other hand, the earth blocks the light from the sun, obscuring the sunlight from directly reaching, and reflecting off of, the moon. When we reflect God's light, we help others find their way to God's kingdom. As Jesus reminded his listeners in the Sermon on the Mount, "You are the light of the world." We are called to be like a city on a hill, whose light cannot be hidden and provides illumination. When we eclipse God's light—that is, when we let ourselves get in the way, like the earth during an eclipse—we obscure God's glory. Instead of reflecting and spreading the light, we diminish the light and promote darkness. My glory or Thy glory? Mine or Thine?

In Jesus, we see the paradox of greatness. In John's Gospel we find that the moment Jesus is glorified, his greatest moment, comes as he hangs on the cross dying for the human race. In laying down his life, we see his glory. We're put off by the person who glorifies himself, who craves the limelight and who works hard to win our praise. We admire the selfless, the self-effacing, the truly humble, the servant.

Joe Delaney, a remarkable young football player, was the AFC Rookie of the Year in 1981. A second-round draft pick by the Kansas City Chiefs, he rushed for 1,121 yards during his first season in the NFL. His second season, in 1982, was impacted by an NFL strike and injuries, but he had already set four franchise records and there was little question that Delaney was the future for the Chiefs. He was an exceptional talent.

It was the off season, June of 1983, and Joe was living in Louisiana. One day he was with friends visiting Chennault Park in Monroe, Louisiana. As he approached a two-acre pond, Delaney saw that there were three children who were struggling and in danger of drowning. Though he did not know how to swim, he dove in to rescue them. One child was saved, but the other two, and Joe, drowned that day.

The impulse to dive in to save these children was characteristic of who Joe Delaney was. President Reagan said of him, "He made the ultimate sacrifice by placing the lives of three children above regard for his own safety. By the supreme example of courage and compassion, this brilliantly gifted young man left a spiritual legacy for his fellow Americans."[7]

"Greater love hath no man than to lay down his life for another."

Delaney was known for putting others first. His high school football coach said of him, "He was always doing something for somebody else."[8] He knew what it was to win accolades and to achieve the glory of a great NFL running back. But he was willing to risk all of that to save the lives of three kids he didn't know, boys ten and eleven years old. The marker on his grave includes these words of Jesus, "Greater love hath no man than to lay down his life for another."

When I pray the doxology of the Lord's Prayer, I'm reminded of Psalm 115:1, a prayer I've prayed many times in the hope that it will shape my heart: "Not to us, Lord, not to us— / no, but to your own name give glory."

Forever. Amen.

The doxology of the Lord's Prayer ends with these two words: forever. Amen. *Forever*, in Greek, is actually three words: *eis tous aionas*, which literally means "into the ages" or "for the eons." We often say that nothing lasts forever. That's true insofar as we mean that our lives and all that is around us are transitory. But there is One whose kingdom, power, and glory actually do last forever, and it is this One we pray and commit our lives as we say this prayer.

In so many ways this prayer is meant to train and prepare us for the forever that lies ahead, the eschatological kingdom of heaven that begins here on earth as we pray and work and live this prayer. As Jesus said, that kingdom is *already* here among us.

But it is also *not yet*. It is still to come. It is a vision that we work toward and pray for, our "preferred picture of the future." But it is more than that. It is what we believe we will taste at death, that realm where God's will is done, the paradise of God.

And, if the vision we read earlier, from Revelation 21, is to be taken in any sense literally, it is what one day will come to earth as it is in heaven:

> *"Look! God's dwelling is here with humankind. He will dwell*
> *with them, and they will be his peoples. God himself will be*
> *with them as their God. He will wipe away every tear from their*
> *eyes. Death will be no more. There will be no mourning, cry-*
> *ing, or pain anymore, for the former things have passed away."*
> *Then the one seated on the throne said, "Look! I'm making all*
> *things new."*
>
> (Revelation 21:3-5)

Jesus's prayer is preparing us for that realm. It is training our minds and hearts for the day when God's kingdom has fully come, and God's will is completely done, where *my* and *mine* has given way to *Thy* and *Thine*. In that place we'll share the bread we need to exist, no one will be hungry for that which gives and sustains life. Freed from guilt and shame, we'll also have released all grudges and resentment. And no longer led into temptation, we will have been completely delivered from evil, darkness, and pain.

This is the forever we're preparing for, the one we pray for in the Lord's Prayer.

Which leads me to its final word: *Amen. Amen* is a Hebrew word, transliterated into Greek and English and many other languages. It literally means, "So be it!" or "May it be so!" What an appropriate ending to the doxology and to the prayer. All of these things we've studied, all that we've prayed for, *Amen. Amen* in your life. *Amen* in mine. *Amen* in the church. Let all God's people say, *AMEN!*

Let's seek to mean what we say and to live these words, as we pray them once more,

Our Father, who art in heaven, hallowed be thy name.
Thy kingdom come, thy will be done on earth as it is in heaven.
Give us this day our daily bread.
And forgive us our trespasses, as we forgive those who trespass
against us.
And lead us, not into temptation, but deliver us from evil.
For thine is the kingdom, and the power, and the glory, forever.
Amen.

POSTSCRIPT
SUGGESTIONS FOR PRAYING THE LORD'S PRAYER

LaVon and I once purchased a king-sized memory foam mattress that was delivered to us by Federal Express. When I looked at the package I thought, "They sent the wrong size, there is no way a twelve-inch deep, king-sized bed fit in that box!" I could not imagine that even a twin mattress would fit inside that relatively small box. But I opened the box, unfolded and spread out the mattress. It had been compressed and vacuum packed with the air removed from the foam. Within a day the mattress had indeed expanded to a king-sized, twelve-inch-deep memory foam mattress.

In some ways the Lord's Prayer is like this. Jesus gave us five very succinct petitions and the early church added a sixth, the doxology. My hope was that this book would open the prayer up to you, to help unfold and expand the depth of meaning it possesses. In this postscript I'll give you a brief example of how I pray the Lord's Prayer each day, as a way of helping you think about using what you've learned in this book while you pray the prayer.

I have found that, using each of the six phrases of the prayer as a starting point, I consider the possible meanings of each phrase as I've shared them with you in this book. As I expand on each word or phrase, I find that it's not hard to spend ten minutes in conversation with God unpacking each of its six petitions. You may not have an hour to devote to praying the Lord's Prayer, so I'll offer a brief version as an example of how I often pray the Lord's Prayer.

Our Father, who art in heaven, hallowed be thy name.

You are not just my Father, you are our *Father*
   Father of those like me and those very different from me,
      Father of those people I love and those I struggle to love.
   Help me remember they are all your children.

You are our Father, *the One who created us, who loves us,*
   who protects us, walks with us, and longs for the best for us;
      The One from whom all blessings have ultimately come.

Father, you hold the entire universe in your hands.
   You are present with the saints who have gone before.
      Yet you are as near as the air that I breathe.

Hallowed be thy *name,*
   not my name, but thy name,
   hallow thy name.
   May others see your majesty, beauty, and love...
      May they see this in my living, in my loving...
      Help me to hallow your name.

Thy kingdom come, thy will be done on earth as it is in heaven.

> *Not my kingdom, but Thy kingdom come.*
> > *May your rule and reign come, in my life, in the lives of your people*
> > > *until it expands and fills the earth.*
> > *I submit to your rule and honor you as my king.*

> *Thy will be done, not mine. Help me to sense your leading.*
> *Help me to long more than anything to do your will.*
> > *May your will be done on earth, not just in my life,*
> > > *but in how we as humans live and love,*
> > > > *just as it is in heaven.*

Give us this day our daily bread.

> *I lift up to you, O Lord, those who don't have enough to eat,*
> > *or who lack the other necessities of life.*
> > *Help me to pay attention,*
> > > *to see and notice those in need.*
> > > > *Please use me, and your church, to generously share with them.*
> *Give me today, dear Lord, the bread I need—your presence, your love.*
> > *Be for me the bread of life today, Lord,*
> > > *and satisfy my hungry heart.*

And forgive us our trespasses, as we forgive those who trespass against us.

> *Lord, forgive me my debts,*
> > *those things I should have done but failed to do*
> > *and those things I should not have done which I did do.*

> *Forgive us Lord, as a race, a people, for the ways in which we have not done your will,*

for the ways in which we have not loved you with our whole heart,
and not loved our neighbor as we love ourselves.
Forgive us for accepting injustice,
for our part in bringing harm to your planet.
Forgive our indifference, our pride, and our lack of empathy forthe suffering of others.

And help me to forgive, as you have forgiven us.
Bless those who have wronged me in the past.
Help me to see my own shortcomings
as I consider the shortcomings of others.
Please help me to let go of the wrongs committed against me
and free me to love even those who wrong me.

And lead us, not into temptation, but deliver us from evil.

Lead me, Lord, today, now, in this moment.
Help me to pay attention to the voice of your Spirit.
I yield my life to you, Lord, do with me what you will.
Lead me away from temptation. You know how easily
I stray from your path, chasing after things that promise pleasure
but only bring pain.
Protect me from evil and the evil one.
Keep me from the path that leads to pain.

And lead us Lord, the human race.
Lead us in our church, in our city, in our state, in our country; lead us in the world.
Help us steer clear of temptation. Lead us away from evil.
And forgive us for the ways we as a people have succumbed to the tempter's lies.

For thine is the kingdom, and the power, and the glory, forever. Amen.

Thine, not mine, is the kingdom, help me to live like it.
Thine, not mine, is the power, help me to yield to it.
Thine, not mine, is the glory, help me to live for your glory.
> *Forever and ever.*
> *So be it!*
> *Amen.*

Use your own words; this is just an example. But I find that by praying the prayer in this way, pondering and expanding upon each word or line, offering myself to God, remembering *ora et labora*, that this prayer is a call to action, helps me to unpack the meaning of this prayer. The Lord's Prayer becomes a meaningful way of yielding my life to God—of praying Thy and Thine, not my and mine. It reminds me to be mindful of others and to forgive others, and to seek their good. I am moved to think in terms of us, ours, and we instead of I, mine, and me.

I'll end with several other suggestions for ways you might use this prayer as a foundation for deepening your spiritual life:

1. Pray the Lord's Prayer daily.

2. Over the course of a week, while you pray it, focus on one of the phrases to meditate upon. In six days you will have covered its six petitions. On Sunday simply pray the entire prayer in worship without a particular emphasis.

3. When you have time, an extended walk, drive, time of exercise, or as you bathe, devote time to praying and meditating upon each of the petitions slowly.

4. Rewrite the prayer in your own words, capturing the same ideas.

5. If you have children or grandchildren, nieces or nephews, teach them the prayer.[1]

6. Spend time in a small group, book club, Sunday school class, or Bible study, reading and studying this book with others.

7. Read and pray the Lord's Prayer as it is found in different translations of Matthew 6.

8. Ask those closest to you to be sure to include this prayer as you approach your own death. You may not be able to say it with them aloud, but you may be able to pray it silently, in your thoughts.

I conclude with one last story of the power of the Lord's Prayer.

The date was July 12, 2016. It was a rainy morning as Amy was driving to work. Traffic was completely stopped. Out of the corner of her eye she could see a large SUV crossing into the median on the divided highway. Picking up speed, it was careening right toward her. She closed her eyes and prayed. When she opened them the bright headlights of this other vehicle were shining right at her, but the car had stopped just shy of hitting her car, its wheels stuck in the mud of the median. Its driver was hunched over the steering wheel.

She jumped out of her car to check on the man. A nurse from the car behind hers ran to the car as well. They opened the door, put the car in park, and examined the man. He was bleeding from a wound to the abdomen and had already lost a great deal of blood. They called 911. The nurse applied pressure to the site of the wound while taking his pulse, then declared, "He's dying." Amy could sense the man's fear as well as her own. She said to me,

> At that moment, the Lord's Prayer came across my heart. I leaned into him, placed my hand on his shoulder, and spoke gently into his ear, "Our Father, who art in heaven, hallowed be thy name. Thy kingdom come, thy will be done on earth as it is in heaven. Give us this day our daily bread. And forgive us our trespasses, as we forgive those who trespass against us. And lead us, not into temptation, but deliver us from evil. For thine is the kingdom, and the power, and the glory, forever. Amen." As I spoke each word, I hovered on them all, slowly and carefully. I was reciting it for him and for me. As I moved through it, his rapid and labored breathing became slower and deeper, until it stopped all together.

She stayed by his side in the pouring rain until the EMS team arrived.

She went on to note that the deceased man's family erected a white cross on the side of the road near the place where he died. She told me, "Each day I pass it, I recite the Lord's Prayer."[2]

On that rainy day, Amy was the presence of Christ for this dying man. And when she could not find the words to say, it was the words that Jesus taught us to pray that came to mind. These were the last words this man would hear this side of eternity, words that seemed to help him find, in his final breaths, peace.

Jesus gave us these words as a gift, to help us know how and what to pray. He gave these words to shape our hearts and

147

lives; inviting us to embrace the love of our Father in heaven and to recall he is as near as the air we breathe. He hoped we might hallow God's name in our everyday lives. He invited us to pray, Thy and Thine, not my and mine. His words beckon us to become the means by which God answers the prayers of others for the bread they need—whether food, or love, or compassion and mercy. He invites us to seek forgiveness from God, but also to extend forgiveness to others. In these sacred words, we ask God to lead us away from the evil we so find ourselves tempted to pursue. And in its powerful doxology, we recognize that the kingdom, the power, and the glory rightly belong to God and not to us.

May these powerful words daily shape our hearts and lives, and through us the world in which we live. Forever. Amen.

Acknowledgments

I've dedicated this book to my grandmother, who first taught me the Lord's Prayer, but I want to acknowledge my mom and dad, who took me to church, where this prayer became forever etched in my memory.

I'm grateful for the people of the United Methodist Church of the Resurrection, for allowing me to serve as their senior pastor these last thirty-one years. The ideas in this book were first shared with them in various sermons on the Lord's Prayer that I have preached over the last three decades. I love this congregation and consider it a great honor and blessing to be their pastor. I am particularly grateful for the sabbatical leave they granted me that made it possible for me to complete this manuscript.

This book would not have been possible without the amazing team at Abingdon Press, including Susan Salley. She is a remarkable person whose collaboration has been invaluable over the years. Thank you, Susan, for your encouragement, vision, and support for my books. And I cannot overstate my gratitude for my editor, Brian Sigmon. Brian took my sermon manuscripts and organized them into a rough draft of this book for me to begin the work of creating the final manuscript. Brian, your editorial suggestions, additions, and subtractions, made this a much better book. Thank you, Brian! I'm deeply grateful for you!

Special thanks to production manager Tim Cobb for overseeing the many corrections and improvements to the final manuscript, and for tirelessly shepherding the book through the production process. I'm deeply appreciative of Alan Vermilye and Elizabeth Pruitt and their ministry in creating interest in the books that Abingdon publishes each year including mine. You are a blessing to me and to every author you work with.

Alongside this book there are small group videos thanks to the amazing team at United Methodist Communications. UMCOM team, you are amazing! I also want to acknowledge the team that develops study guides for children, youth, and adults so that congregations can study *The Lord's Prayer* together. Thank you, each of you, for the outstanding work you've done in preparing these excellent guides.

I'm also grateful for Kevin and Kristen Howdeshell for their beautiful illustrations in the children's book *The Most Important Prayer of All: Stella Learns the Lord's Prayer*, and to Tracey Craddock, Laura Lockhart, and the rest of the Abingdon team who worked to make this book and the children's book possible.

I want to thank my best friend and partner of forty years, LaVon Bandy Hamilton. She endured days and nights alone while I was working on completing this manuscript. Her insights and musings shaped my own thoughts as I wrote. We have prayed this prayer many times together, and it has shaped our life together and our marriage. Thank you, LaVon, for your love and care and encouragement. I so love you.

Finally, I want to thank Stella Louise Hamilton Slate, my now seven-year-old granddaughter, for allowing me to write a children's book about her learning the Lord's Prayer and for the way she has reminded me of the love of God for each of us. Stella, Papa loves you more than you can possibly know!

NOTES

Introduction

1   Since 1611, scholars have found earlier copies of the various New Testament books including Codex Sinaiticus, a complete New Testament and major portions of the Old Testament dating from the 300s found at St. Catherine's Monastery at Mt. Sinai in 1844, and Codex Vaticanus, also from the 300s, which while known when the King James was translated, was not studied and its value recognized until the late 1800s.

2   *The Apostolic Fathers*, Volume I, translated by Kirsopp Lake (Loeb Classical Library No. 24).

1. Our Father, Who Art in Heaven, Hallowed Be Thy Name

1   Roberta Bondi, *A Place to Pray: Reflections on the Lord's Prayer* (Nashville, TN: Abingdon Press, 1998), 22-23.

2. Whose Will Be Done?

1   Daniel J. Harrington, S. J., *The Gospel of Matthew*, Sacra Pagina series (Collegeville, MN: Liturgical Press, 1991), 95.

2   Jonathan T. Pennington, "The Kingdom of God in the Gospel of Matthew," *Southern Baptist Journal of Theology*, 12:1, Spring 2008, p. 47, italics in original. See also his excellent book, *Heaven and Earth in the Gospel of Matthew* (Grand Rapids, MI: Baker Academic, 2007).

3   The one exception to this is in John 9, where Jesus heals a man who was born blind. The disciples asked Jesus, "Who sinned so that he was born blind, this man or his parents?" Jesus responds, "Neither he nor his parents. This happened so that God's mighty works might be displayed in him." There the question is whether Jesus was teaching that God had made this man to be born blind and live blind throughout his entire life just for

this moment, or if Jesus was making a broader statement, that the man's blindness was not the result of sin (as was commonly assumed of illness in first-century Judaism), but that it (and by implication all other sickness and tragedy) was an opportunity for God's work to be seen.

4   William Willimon and Stanley Hauerwas, *Lord, Teach Us: The Lord's Prayer & the Christian Life* (Nashville, TN: Abingdon Press, 1996), 50.

5   Frederick Dale Brunner, *Matthew: A Commentary*. Volume 1: The Christbook, Matthew 1-12. Revised and Expanded Edition (Grand Rapids, MI: Eerdmans, 2004), 302.

3. Our Daily Bread

1   Translation from the Jewish Virtual Library at https://www .jewishvirtuallibrary.org/the-shema, accessed August 4, 2021.

2   "HHS Poverty Guidelines for 2021," https://aspe.hhs.gov/poverty -guidelines, accessed August 4, 2021.

3   "Food Security and Nutrition Assistance," https://www.ers.usda.gov/data -products/ag-and-food-statistics-charting-the-essentials/food-security-and -nutrition-assistance/, accessed August 5, 2021.

4   IMF Country Report No. 17/184 on Malawi. Published in July 2017.

5   Willimon and Hauerwas, *Lord, Teach Us*, 73.

6   You can read more about Jeff's story, see his art, and watch video interviews with him, at https://jeffhansonart.com, accessed August 6, 2021.

4. Forgive . . . As We Forgive

1   "KIDS IN CHURCH" joke, http://www.jokebuddha.com /Forgive#ixzz5QAJaXF4I, accessed August 6, 2021.

2   "KIDS AND PRAYER / CHURCH," http://funehumor.com/fun_doc 6/fun_0637.shtml, accessed August 6, 2021.

3   "The association of anger and hostility with future coronary heart disease," https://pubmed.ncbi.nlm.nih.gov/19281923/, accessed August 6, 2021.

4   Adam Hamilton, *Forgiveness: Finding Peace Through Letting Go* (Nashville, TN: Abingdon Press, 2012).

5   Robin Casarjian, as quoted in "Conversations About Forgiveness: Participant Handbook" (Fetzer Institute, Kalamazoo, MI), https://fetzer .org/resources/conversations-about-forgiveness-participant-guide.

6   "Forgive to Live: Forgiveness, Health, and Longevity," Loren L. Toussaint, Amy D. Owen, and Alyssa Cheadle, Journal of Behavioral Medicine, February 2005, Vol. 28, No. 1, https://www.academia.edu/1007805 /Forgive_to_Live_Forgiveness_Health_and_Longevity, accessed August 7, 2021.

7   Seven Days of Kindness, https://givesevendays.org, accessed August 7, 2021.

8   Paul Tillich, "To Whom Much Is Forgiven," *The New Being* (New York: Scribner's, 1955), 9.

5. And Lead Us, Not into Temptation...

1   I cannot recall where I heard this joke and I've been unable to find it online. Among my sources of jokes is Dr. Clayton Smith, retired United Methodist pastor, and it may have been from him. My apologies for failing to give a more specific attribution of this bit of humor.

2   Thomas A. Dorsey, "Precious Lord, Take My Hand," *The United Methodist Hymnal* (Nashville, TN: The United Methodist Publishing House, 1989), 474. © 1938 Hill & Range Songs, Inc., renewed Unichappell Music. Inc.

3   E. W. Blandy, "Where He Leads Me," *The United Methodist Hymnal*, 338.

4   C. H. Spurgeon, *Spiritual Warfare in a Believer's Life* (Lynnwood, WA: Emerald Books, 1993), 64.

6. For THINE Is the Kingdom, Power, and Glory

1   Willimon and Hauerwas, *Lord, Teach Us*, 96.

2   Charles Colson, *Kingdoms in Conflict* (Grand Rapids, MI: Zondervan, 1987), 174.

3   André Pierre Colombat, "Weapons of the Spirit," from *The Holocaust in French Film* (Lanham, MD: Scarecrow Press, 1993). https://www.chambon.org/weapons_colombat1_en.htm, accessed August 8, 2021. (See also, Hal Hinson, "Weapons of the Spirit," *The Washington Post*, January 19, 1990. https://www.washingtonpost.com/wp-srv/style/longterm/movies/videos/weaponsofthespiritnrhinson_a0a92f.htm), accessed August 8, 2021. I am indebted to my editor for sharing this story with me.

4   Colson, *Kingdoms in Conflict*, 175.

5   Colson, *Kingdoms in Conflict*, 273.

6   "Lord Acton's Letter to Archbishop Mandell Creighton," https://history.hanover.edu/courses/excerpts/165acton.html, accessed August 9, 2021.

7   "On This Day in Sports," http://onthisdayinsports.blogspot.com/2013/06/june-29-1983-joe-delaney-of-kansas-city.html, accessed August 8, 2021.

8   Sarah Crawford, "Haughton hero, NFL star Joe Delaney died 35 years ago," *Shreveport Times*, June 29, 2018. https://www.shreveporttimes.com/story/news/2018/06/29/haughton-hero-nfl-star-joe-delaney-died-35-years-ago/741928002/, accessed August 8, 2021.

Postscript: Suggestions for Praying the Lord's Prayer

1 I have written a children's book aimed at helping parents and grandparents, aunts, and uncles to teach the prayer to children. See *The Most Important Prayer of All: Stella Learns the Lord's Prayer* (Nashville, TN: Abingdon, 2021).

2 I'm grateful for Amy Barber Park for sharing her story with me. I found it a deeply moving picture of the power of the Lord's Prayer, and of her willingness to act as the presence of Christ for this man as he died.

WATCH VIDEOS BASED ON *THE LORD'S PRAYER: THE MEANING AND POWER OF THE PRAYER JESUS TAUGHT* WITH ADAM HAMILTON THROUGH AMPLIFY MEDIA.

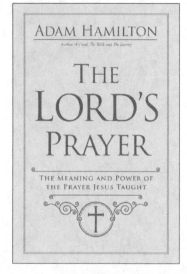

Amplify Media is a multimedia platform that delivers high quality, searchable content with an emphasis on Wesleyan perspectives for churchwide, group, or individual use on any device at any time. In a world of sometimes overwhelming choices, Amplify gives church leaders and congregants media capabilities that are contemporary, relevant, effective and, most importantly, affordable and sustainable.

With **Amplify Media** church leaders can:

- Provide a reliable source of Christian content through a Wesleyan lens for teaching, training, and inspiration in a customizable library
- Deliver their own preaching and worship content in a way the congregation knows and appreciates
- Build the church's capacity to innovate with engaging content and accessible technology
- Equip the congregation to better understand the Bible and its application
- Deepen discipleship beyond the church walls

Ⅱ AMPLIFY. MEDIΛ

Ask your group leader or pastor about Amplify Media and sign up today at www.AmplifyMedia.com.